a Brush
with Death

SUNY series in Modern Jewish Literature and Culture
Sarah Blacher Cohen, editor

Morris Wyszogrod

a Brush with Death

an artist in the death camps

State University of New York Press

Published by
State University of New York Press, Albany

© 1999 State University of New York

For information, address State University of New York Press
State University Plaza, Albany, New York 12246

Cover design by Morris Wyszogrod
Illustrations done after the liberation by Morris Wyszogrod
Production by Dana Foote
Marketing by Dana Yanulavich

Library of Congress Cataloging-in-Publication Data
Wyszogrod, Morris, 1920–
    A brush with death : an artist in the death camps / Morris
Wyszogrod.
        p.   cm. — (SUNY series in modern Jewish literature and
culture)
    Includes index.
    ISBN 0–7914–4313–2 (hc : alk. paper). — ISBN 0–7914–4314–0 (pb :
alk. paper)
    1. Wyszogrod, Morris, 1920–   . 2. Jews—Poland—Warsaw—
Biography.   3. Holocaust, Jewish (1939–1945)—Poland—Warsaw—
Personal narratives.   4. Holocaust, Jewish (1939–1945), in art.
5. Warsaw (Poland)—Biography.   I. Title.   II. Series: SUNY series
on modern Jewish literature and culture.
DS135.P63W946   1999
940.53'18'092—dc21
    [B]   99–27877
                                                               CIP

10   9   8   7   6   5   4   3   2

In memory of my beloved parents,
Doba and Chaim Boruch Wyszogrod,
my sister, Esther Raizl,
my brothers, Pesach and Shlomo Yitzhak—
and all those
who perished with no one to mourn them.

Acknowledgments

First and foremost, credit must go to my dear wife, Helen, my most devoted life's partner. For years, she, together with our children Diane and Barry, listened to my story, and heard my message: Remember! Do not forget! They went through the passage of pain with me. To them, I say, thank you.

I am deeply indebted to Professors Edith and Michael Wyschogrod for their encouragement and support, and for making it possible for me to tell publicly the story of my survival.

Professor Michael Wyschogrod was unique in spending many long hours listening to my descriptions of the pilgrimage of destruction of my family and our people. He steadfastly stayed with me on this terrible journey through the gates of Hell, and I thank him for that, and for his tireless efforts in preparing the original transcript.

I am grateful to Professor Edith Wyschogrod who first brought my story to the attention of the editorial staff at State University of New York Press. I want to express my sincere thanks to Mr. James Peltz, senior editor at SUNY Press, for his interest and efforts in publishing my memoir.

Finally, my daughter, Diane Wyshogrod Zlotogorski, devoted all her strength and talent to editing my story. Ours was an unforgettable partnership. We read and reread, wrote and rewrote, laughed and cried together. All along, she never stopped insisting that I tell my story in my own words, in my own way.

Prologue

Spring, 1942, in the Warsaw Ghetto, the third year of the war. Passover was approaching, and as always, it was time to prepare for the holiday of our deliverance. But we had nothing to prepare.

The evening of Pesach came. The whole family gathered in the kitchen, where the single window was sealed with rags so no light would shine outside and give us away. From the street we heard horrible screams. The Germans had entered the ghetto and there was a bloodbath. Starving children begging in the streets were being shot by the mighty German patrols.

We had placed the table, which usually stood against the wall, in the middle of the narrow room. It was covered with a white tablecloth, with the five-branched candelabrum standing in the center, a dead witness; there were no candles. My mother had set the table just as she always did, with our special Pesach dishes, white porcelain plates with a floral border. She had made sure that all the dishes and utensils had been properly *kashered* (prepared for Passover use). The Haggadahs lay in front of us.

My father sat at the head of the table, his back to the window. To his right sat my brother Pesach, and then my brother Shlomo. To my father's left sat my sister Esther Raizl, then my mother. I sat at the opposite end of the table in order to be able to help my mother at the big white-tiled stove to my right. The only light we had came from a single homemade carbide lamp, which gave off a flickering blue glow. In its faint light, the images moved as if in a devilish dance.

My father stood up, raised a glass of water, and made kiddush over it. I thought of the hungry who, by tradition, are invited to share this meal. But the plates remained empty— there was no matzo. Under these severe conditions, the holiday took on ominous overtones. From minute to minute, it became more anxious and more depressing. I helped my mother serve the meal: water boiled with coarse black salt and some rotten cabbage leaves, whatever we'd been able to find.

My father continued reading from the Haggadah. He wanted so much to believe that the miracle of our people's deliverance from Egypt would occur for us too. He tried to infuse the Seder with hope, that maybe next year the redemption would come, and we would celebrate and be free. To the last moment, he believed with all his might that some miracle would occur and we would be spared from death. He tried to convey this to us. "Children," he said, "don't fall into despair."

He motioned to us to open the door for the traditional arrival of Elijah the Prophet. One of the children usually opened the door for Elijah, but we were all sitting at the table, motionless. My mother got up to open the door, and my father began to recite the *Shfoch Chamoscho,* the passage in the Haggadah entreating God: "Pour out Your wrath on the nations who do not acknowledge You."

My father's *Shfoch Chamoscho* was the most powerful curse I ever heard in my life. It was his rage, his hatred, his belief that the enemy could be mortally wounded with his words. He hurled it at the enemy with all his remaining strength, the last breaths of life left to a man dying in agony.

At that moment, his curse was also mine. I too was killing the enemy. This was the only way I could express how I felt under these helpless circumstances. How much more could we take, how much pain and disaster, how much shooting, killing, screams in the middle of the night? The Angel of Death was strangling us, destroying us. My family was dying right in front of me, and I could do nothing to help them, to save them. The only thing left was my father's curse, this final outcry of a person preparing for death.

The horror of my family's last Passover stays with me. *Haya, hoveh, v'yihiyeh.* It was, it is, and it will continue to be. I never forgot. I will never forget. I will never forgive them for what they did to us, and I will continue to remember forever and ever.

The *Shfoch Chamoscho* was finished. I looked around the table. My brother Pesach looked half dead. He was slumped over the table, his chin hooked over its edge, his hands hanging down by his sides to the floor. Shlomo, sitting next to him, and my sister, across the table, were exhausted. They looked like skeletons, their faces, ash gray. Their legs were like matches, like narrow pipes, with big balloons below the ankles where fluid accumulated. My father's face was unshaven, a sure sign of demoralization; he still had his razor, and one razor blade, which we all shared, passing it from hand to hand.

I carried them into their beds, piled them all together. We slept close to one another for warmth, in beds pulled together, under the few blankets we had left.

1

I was born on April 20. April 20 was also Hitler's birthday. This coincidence would someday almost cost me my life.

But when my life began, on 2 Iyar 5681, there was no hint of the shadows that would fall later on. I was welcomed into a home of warmth and hospitality. My family had to struggle to make ends meet, but so did everyone else around us. And there was so much love and commotion within our immediate and extended family and friends, that it more than made up for what we lacked. Our days were full of life, and music, and art.

My father, Chaim Boruch Wyszogród, was a professional musician. He was born in Lublin in 1885, the third of four children, the son of an egg dealer, Mordechai (after whom my middle name was taken) and Raizl. My father came from a traditional Jewish home and studied in a yeshiva. He also received a secular education. If he had any musical talent as a child, it apparently was neither recognized nor developed. It lay dormant until he was about seventeen or eighteen, when he left his parents, his brothers Hirsh Baer and Josef, and sister Basia, and came to Warsaw to seek his fortune. What he found was music.

My father fell in love with the clarinet and the drums. He began studying music, supporting himself by working in a jewelry factory, first as an apprentice chain maker and eventually being promoted to supervisor. He served as a secretary in the union of jewelry shop workers. This role fit him because he had a strong social conscience and always stood up for justice. He was a very good-natured person with tremendous compassion for the poor and helpless. I remember him walking around Warsaw collecting money from his friends for those in need. Years later, after the war, I met a Mr. Gabriel Braun who had been an apprentice in the jewelry factory where my father had been a supervisor. In contrast to some supervisors who mistreated their apprentices, my father had treated him well and even helped him immigrate to America. In gratitude, Mr. Braun sent my father an affidavit in 1921 so that my family too could apply for immigration to the United States. My parents were unable to use it, however, because the Polish quota to America was very restrictive. The affidavit lay around the house, useless.

His musical education completed, my father left the factory and became a professional musician. He was a member of the National Union of Polish Musicians and was highly respected. He first performed with the orchestras of Jewish theater companies, such as the famous Esther Rachel Kaminska Jewish Theater. Later, he played with major Polish orchestras including the Warsaw Philharmonic. Although he began his career as a clarinetist, by the early 1920s, he began

Doba Blajfeder Wyszogrod, ca. 1911, the author's mother, a millinery and theatrical costume designer, wearing a costume and hat of her own design

to have difficulty blowing the clarinet and switched to percussion instruments.

My mother, Doba Blajfeder, was born in Warsaw in 1890, the daughter of Moshe Halevi ben Yekutiel Blajfeder and Esther Gincel. Moshe (after whom I was named) owned a kosher butcher shop, and was a member of the Jewish Burial Society, a prestigious status in the Jewish community. Doba had an older brother, Mendel. Esther Gincel died of pneumonia at the age of twenty-nine, when my mother was two and a half years old. Her father remarried, and, with his new wife, Chana Riva, had eight children, with whom my mother was very close.

The entire family squeezed into a two-room apartment at 32 Dzielna Street in the Jewish section of Warsaw, one building away from the Pawiak prison and across the street from the Saint Augustine Church, two local landmarks. My mother continued to live there after her parents died, around 1917, and after she married my father in 1918. I was born in this apartment in 1920, as was my sister Esther Raizl, in 1922, and my brother Pesach, in 1925.

When I was seven years old, we moved around the corner to a slightly bigger apartment at 48 Pawia Street. The new apartment, number 18, was on the third floor, overlooking the street. It had a kitchen, a living room with its floor-to-ceiling tiled oven and little balcony, and one bedroom. Just before the kitchen was the toilet, with a little enclosure where we stored coal. My youngest brother, Shlomo Yitzhak, was born in this apartment in 1927.

Even before the war, conditions at home were tough. We had only cold running water and had to bathe in a big wooden wash basin in the kitchen, with water heated on the stove. As a child, I almost prayed to get sick in order to get an orange or a pineapple, fruit that was too expensive to be served except at the most special of occasions. I shared a bed with my brothers. We had no mattresses, but slept on large sacks filled with straw and covered with a heavy blanket and sheets. Every year before Passover, the peasants would come to replace the old straw, which had become fully compressed and stone-hard, with fresh, new straw, which smelled wonderful. We had heavy feather-filled comforters for the winter, and huge feather pillows. No one suffered from hiatus hernia from sleeping too low; you were practically sitting up when you slept.

Despite the difficult conditions, life was quite interesting for a little boy with a ready band of adventurers, both siblings and friends from the neighborhood. Sometimes, when my mother got fed up with all the noise we made, she would chase us out of the apartment, shaking the rug beater at us. We'd march down to the street with me in the lead, like a mother duck, and all the other children—my brothers and sister, and our friends—falling in line behind me, like ducklings. They called me *Di Mame*. We would march around the neighborhood, which, with all the poverty and hunger, still bubbled with energy and activity, warmth and caring, curses and laughter. There was always something to see. The Pawiak prison with its big chimney (they ran a laundry on the premises) fascinated us. Before the war, political prisoners were jailed there, with female inmates held in a section known as "Serbia." (The prison became notorious later during the German occupation as a place of imprisonment, torture, and execution of Polish and Jewish prisoners alike.) We'd visit the fire department a few blocks away. We had no playground, so we sometimes played in the yard of the Saint Augustine Church across the street. When we were particularly daring, we would sneak into the chapel to peek at the dead bodies laid out before a funeral. Some of the corpses were dressed so nicely, I thought they looked better than when they had been alive.

Then there were street performers—a few musicians with an accordion, a tuba, a banjo, a violinist—who made their way through the Jewish sector, playing the romantic songs of the day, especially the tango. Small, local circuses would spread big blankets on the sidewalk, announce their arrival with a crash of music, and start performing acrobatic

The Wyszogrod Family, 1930, photographs the author saved throughout the years in the concentration camps.
Top: Youngest brother Shlomo Yitzhak
Sitting left to right: Brother Pesach, Morris, sister Esther Raizl
Right: Parents, Doba and Chaim Boruch

tricks. Often they hired local beggar children to perform with them or work the crowd for handouts. The performers collected small gifts of money or tiny wrapped packages of food that the onlookers threw down from their windows before moving on down the street to their next performance. There was even a school for thieves, safecrackers, and pickpockets in the neighborhood, on Gęsia Street, a few blocks away. One day, I heard wild screams coming from a woman who lived on one of the floors below us. Apparently, someone had been trying to pick her lock. Then I heard a response: "*Baleboste,* Lady, give him a break, the kid's gotta learn somehow!"

With so many aunts and uncles, I could always count on someone having some special treat for me. My mother's youngest brother, my uncle Boruch, was very sweet to me. He ran a small candy store. I loved going there because he would give me ice cream, my choice of chocolate, vanilla, or lemon. He had glass jars of cherry, lemon, or strawberry syrup. My favorite was cherry. He'd spoon a little bit into a glass, add a spritz of soda water, and I was in heaven. He also used to put me on the frame of his bicycle and drive me all over the city. I loved it.

My beloved cousin, Mordechai Leib, son of my father's older brother Josef, lived with us while he studied to become a tailor at the ORT school. He always gave me a bar of chocolate, and kept me supplied with flashlights and batteries, which I was crazy about. I used to try to speed up the day and bring on the night by hiding under a blanket just so I could use my flashlight.

Sometimes, my uncle Hershel took us to the beach on the Vistula River on Saturday afternoons. We would walk over with him and his two little boys, Moshe and David, taking some sandwiches and drinks. I enjoyed watching the river and the steamboats with their big paddlewheels and the steam puffing out of their tall chimneys. The most popular boat was the *Bajka,* meaning fairy tale. In summer, an orchestra would play and people danced on deck, below the big Polish flag flying from the bow. (Later, my school used to take us for rides on this boat on various school holidays.)

During the late 1920s and especially in the 1930s following the Depression, when the economic situation worldwide was bad for everyone, Jews in Poland also had to contend with anti-Semitism. Competition among performing musicians was intense and jobs were often given first to non-Jews. In order to supplement his dwindling income as a performer, my father started giving music lessons, teaching clarinet, drums, glockenspiel, xylophone, and vibraphone. In addition, he gradually developed a business of importing, selling, renting, and repairing musical instruments.

The business was run out of our apartment. Violins, Hawks trumpets from Britain, Selmer saxophones, drums of all sizes, were hanging all over the house. Our workplace was the kitchen. We had drills, pliers, wires, all kinds of bits of brass, copper, nickel, a polisher to polish the finished pieces of metal, even a special thread cutter for preparing precision-fitted screws for the instruments. We had special wooden and metal inserts, which were used to reshape dented brass instruments. My mother, who was artistic and very handy with tools, gave up designing and repairing theatrical clothing and millinery to help my father in his growing music business. One of her specialties was making the felt-tipped heads of drumsticks for the kettledrums.

From the time I was about ten years old, I too was repairing instruments, doing whatever needed to be done. I learned how to apply little white leather finger pads to the wind instruments, how to fit new drum skins or repair old, torn ones, for the snare drums as well as the great big kettledrums. I competed with Ludwig, an American company, making drum foot pedals. I learned how to fix violins from a Polish master craftsman whose shop was not far from us. He specialized in violins, violas, and cellos.

Another master craftsman, Mr. Lewitan, a concertmaster of the bass fiddle, taught me how to repair violin bows. I was even better at this than my father because I was extremely handy and not intimidated by handling high-quality violins. In 1934, the famous violinist Bronisław Huberman (who later helped establish the Israel Philharmonic) visited Warsaw. He had damaged one of his bows and needed someone to fix it. He was referred to us and I repaired it. He even gave me a two zloty tip.

Having all those instruments at home was irresistible. When we were a little older, in the early 1930s, we organized little musical bands. Pesach played the trumpet, and sometimes the drums. Shlomo played the cymbals. Esther Raizl didn't play any instruments but she liked to sing. I played various instruments mainly by ear: the accordion, the clarinet, the banjo, or the mandolin, my favorite. None of us was interested in being a musician, we just wanted to blow the hell out of the instruments and have a good time. My uncles and aunts used to come up and visit with their children. Neighborhood kids dropped in. All the kids wanted to get their hands on the instruments, and we would create a symphony orchestra. We used to make such music that, from all the windows around us, neighbors would start screaming that we should shut up.

Our house was always filled with music. We didn't have a real radio, just a crystal radio with earphones. It picked up only local transmissions from Warsaw stations or the national Polish station. Later, my aunt Pesa bought a big Phillips short-

Author's brothers; *left,* Shlomo 2 and Pesach 4

wave radio which received transmissions from all over the world. It was a special treat to go to her house and listen to her radio.

We had a gramophone and a few records: operas, Yiddish songs imported from America like *Di Yidishe Mame,* and jazz. My favorite was Louis Armstrong. The music in his voice made me laugh.

There were always musicians hanging around our house. My father became a kind of patron of Warsaw musicians who nicknamed him *Ojczulek* (Father). Our home served as a meeting place where information about job opportunities was traded. Jobless musicians would borrow instruments they couldn't afford to buy in order to be able to accept jobs. My father was always ready to listen to someone's troubles and offer his advice when asked. I remember my parents discussing with Roman Szulc, chief timpanist for the Warsaw Philharmonic (my mother made drumsticks for him), his invitation from the great conductor Sergei Koussevitsky to join the Boston Philharmonic in 1935. My father supported his decision to go, and we all went to the Warsaw Central Railway Station to see him off with his family.

My mother saw to it that there was always something to eat when people dropped in. There was often a big pot of potato or lima bean soup—my favorite—with bits of flour fried in chicken fat thrown into it. The large table in the living room was always set with a pot of tea, bread and marmalade, or cake. For some of these unemployed musicians, this was a rare chance to satisfy their hunger.

Many musician friends would gather at our house on Sundays to play together: quartets, quintets, and everything else, both classical and popular music. I would listen in envy: how they could play! At these gatherings, my father often played the xylophone. Lewitan, who'd taught me to restring violin bows, played the bass fiddle, which was taller than he was. He was a skinny, bald man in his seventies, with a great mustache that had turned yellow under his nose from constant pipe smoking and became white toward the ends. Our next-door neighbors, the Szermans, were also professional musicians. The oldest son, Tsałke, the accordionist, loved French songs, tangos, and fox trots. Sholem played the violin. Aaron, the youngest, played the trumpet and other brass instruments at one of Warsaw's fanciest nightclubs, the Adria. A close family friend, Izak Mandelbaum, specialized in cabaret music, and played the clarinet, saxophone, and accordion, as well as the piano. One violinist, Moshe Rigman, was nicknamed *Der Geyler Paltn* (The Yellow Overcoat). He always wore an overcoat and would hook his violin on a button under his coat, so that he could fill his empty violin case and his pockets with leftovers from whatever party he played at, to bring home to his wife and four children. He would come up to enjoy a tea, play a little, tell a few jokes. Then there was Simcha, "the mobile cafeteria." A proud individual, he carried his own piece of black bread wrapped in a piece of paper in his pocket, a lump of sugar, and a double-spoon filled with tea. All he asked for was hot water to make his tea, and a chance to sit down and report about his activities. I remember Lustman, a jazz drummer who juggled his drumsticks while playing, never missing a beat. He would show up with his girlfriend, a professional magician who had appeared with the famous Polish traveling Staniewski Circus in Warsaw. My brothers, sister, and I would line up around the table, waiting for the magic show. She threw eggs into the air, made them disappear and then reappear, unbroken. She juggled cards, pulled animals out of her top hat, and we burst into laughter. She kept promising to tell us all her secrets.

Izak Mandelbaum left Poland for Palestine before the war. None of the rest of these people survived. For them, the music ended in Treblinka.

My father was on good terms with non-Jewish musicians as well; artists in general tended to be more liberal than the general population. I remember several of them visiting us, always elegant, bowing and kissing my mother's hand, Polish style. Eugeniusz Mossakowski, baritone of the Warsaw Opera, wanted his son to become a musician and my father lent him some instruments. Zofia Wierchowska, a skinny, elegant, blue-eyed woman in her late thirties, was a drummer,

13

performing in nightclubs. She rented a whole set of drums from my father. Wiktor Tychowski, whose specialty was the Hawaiian guitar, and Lawrusiewicz, the Polish Segovia, also dropped in from time to time.

Knowing all these musicians had an extra benefit. The biggest fun I had was going to the movies or the theater. But tickets were too expensive. Sometimes I would wait at the stage entrances of theaters until the musicians came, and would sneak in with them and sit in some corner of the orchestra pit. The only disadvantage was that I sat right under the stage or screen, and had to strain my neck, looking up to see the action. (At other times, a whole group of us would sneak around to the back of the theater where one of the ushers let all of us in for a tip of one or two zlotys.)

My father got along well with all types of people, from all walks of life. He moved in rather bohemian circles without fully belonging to any of them. He saw many Jews drift away from religion into socialism because of the bitter poverty, and he himself leaned toward the left-wing Poale Zion (the Labor Zionist Movement). However, he maintained his religious beliefs and traditional ways, which was somewhat unusual for a musician; many of the Jewish musicians in Warsaw were more assimilated, some had converted, some had intermarried.

My parents came from religious homes and our home was a traditional one. We kept kosher and my father did not work on the Sabbath. (In high school, I had to attend class on Saturday, and would walk out of my neighborhood quietly early in the morning so as not to offend anyone's religious sensibilities.) We regularly attended a *chevreh*, a small synagogue called *Ahavath Achim* at 49 Nalewki Street. After the turmoil of the week, I loved going with my friends to the nearby House of Study at 22 Pawia Street on Friday night after the Sabbath meal. I enjoyed listening to the men discuss the Torah and debate various interpretations of the Talmud.

We were a very close-knit family. We were always visiting each other on Saturday afternoons, drinking glasses of tea with big lumps of sugar, singing special Sabbath melodies, with my uncles improvising harmonies.

Every year, before the start of Yom Kippur, all my aunts and uncles (my mother's brothers and sisters) would gather at our house to wish each other a happy New Year. There were lots of tears, and reminiscences of the people we had lost throughout the years, and asking forgiveness if anyone had offended anyone. We placed big candles, about twenty-four inches tall and an inch and a half thick, in brass holders set in a box of sand on the table, and each departed family member was remembered with a candle. (This was in the better days. Later we had to save, and only two large candles stood, representing all the departed.) Then everyone would leave, we would prepare for Yom Kippur, eat our meal, and go to the synagogue.

Our family's closeness made it that much harder when the economic situation sometimes forced some of my relatives to seek a better life elsewhere. In 1929, my mother's older brother, Mendel, left for the United States with his wife and three children. My cousin Mordechai Leib moved to Montevideo, Uruguay. (I tried to trace him later, but never found him.) My uncle Boruch left Poland because he got lucky: he won 5,000 zlotys in the Polish National Lottery in 1938, when he was thirty-four. He and a few friends, all living under miserable circumstances, made a vow to stick together and go to Argentina, where there was a demand for workers. They left their wives and children behind until they could establish themselves there.

My father's dream was that someday there would be a Jewish land. I remember when the Revisionist leader, Zev Jabotinsky, came to speak in Warsaw—I was about fourteen at the time. He gave a fiery speech, exhorting us to leave the diaspora and go to fight for our Jewish homeland. A number of our friends, including Izak Mandelbaum, the cabaret musician, did leave for Palestine. I also always assumed that my future would not be in Poland, that I would eventually make my way either to Palestine as well, or to America, to rejoin my uncle Mendel.

2

My parents' greatest desire was to make sure that we children got a good education. They were my first teachers, teaching me the Hebrew and Latin alphabets by the time I was about three or four years old. We spoke Yiddish at home, but were fluent in Polish as well. When I was ready for elementary school, my parents sent me to the private Aaron Krelman School, which offered a double curriculum: Jewish subjects taught in Hebrew and Yiddish, and secular subjects taught in Polish. To pay for school, my parents often had to obtain loans from loansharks and pawn my mother's engagement and wedding rings and other valuables.

The subject that made the most impression on me in elementary school was Jewish history. My teacher, Rabbi Jacob Ackerman, described the tragedy of the Jewish people, their wanderings, the pogroms, and particularly, their suffering during the Spanish Inquisition. This left a deep mark on my soul. Who could imagine that one day I myself would live through the worst Inquisition of all?

The school only went up to the fourth grade. Then I was transferred to a public school at 68 Nowolipki Street where most of the teachers and students were Jewish because it was located in the Jewish section of the city. (Dr. Emmanuel Ringelblum's Warsaw ghetto chronicles were later found under the ruins of this very building.) My Jewish education continued at home with private tutors. One of them was my father's cousin, Josef Dov Flamm, a Hebrew scholar. He had been the principal of a Hebrew school in Lubicz, Poland, but was forced to close the school and flee due to anti-Semitic attacks by locals. My father brought him and his family to Warsaw where he supported himself by giving private lessons.

I always loved to draw. I remember once seeing my father off at the railway station when he traveled with the orchestra to perform. I was thrilled by the sight of the puffing locomotive and the long string of cars. When I returned home with my mother, I started to draw locomotives and trains. I was four years old.

As far back as elementary school, I dreamed of becoming an artist. I was inspired by two people. The first was my uncle Itzchak, one of my mother's brothers. A scribe by profession, he was always busy repairing Torah scrolls, calligraphing liturgical texts, and writing letters for people who were illiterate. The second was Naphtali Baron, a painter friend of my father's, who painted signs to supplement his income. I loved to watch him paint and do lettering. He often gave me paint, brushes, and paper to work with.

During my last year of public school, my parents and I discussed my future education and career. We agreed that the best choice would be graphic arts, a practical profession in the arts, which was close to my heart and talent. I could earn a living, and eventually be able to realize my dream of immigrating either to Palestine or America.

It became my great ambition to become a student of the Marshal Józef Piłsudski School of Graphics in Warsaw. The school featured a complete academic curriculum in addition to teaching creative graphic design and printing methods (lithography, typesetting, and engraving). The school was unique, the only one of its kind in Poland. Unfortunately, being a Jew in that school was unique as well. Only a handful of Jews had been graduated from the school since its establishment in 1926.

It was very difficult to be accepted to this school. I had to demonstrate great patriotism, and pass a three-day exam which tested my knowledge of mathematics, Polish history and literature, my views about Poland, and my skills in poster design and drawing. My acceptance, in 1936, was a tremendous achievement for me, both personally and as a Jew. Every Jewish student admitted to this school was known to the Jewish community because it was so rare. There were three other Jews in my class besides me: Itzchak Kornblum (later killed in one of the first German air raids on Warsaw), Amram Warszawski, son of the well-known Hebrew writer Yakir Warszawski, and Bolesław Engelman (both of whom perished with their families in Treblinka).

Sending me to such a school involved great financial sacrifice for my parents. It cost twenty-five zlotys a month just for me, in addition to the cost of my brothers' and sister's tuitions. Once again, my parents pawned some of their belongings to cover the cost. In addition, a Polish musician named Bronisław Bykowski, who was very devoted to my father, pawned his and his wife's wedding rings to help us.

Bykowski was also an amateur photographer, and it was he who took the beautiful photograph of us four kids, the quartet, which I was to carry with me throughout the war.

The years I spent in the graphic school were very productive and rewarding. The double curriculum was rigorous. I attended school six days a week, eight hours a day including Saturday, when we only studied until about 2 P.M. We covered all the usual subjects: mathematics, geography, Polish literature and history, chemistry, and physics. In addition, we received a thorough grounding in graphic arts, both the creative aspects of art and design, and the technology of preparing designs for mass reproduction. We studied typesetting, engraving, printing, lithography, offset printing, and rotogravure. I was privileged to study under Poland's foremost paper sculptor, Professor Tadeusz Lipski, who taught me graphic design, three-dimensional design, and paper sculpture.

Despite the anti-Semitism that existed in Poland during those years, the atmosphere at the Marshal Piłsudski School was liberal and tolerant based on ethical and democratic principles. I enjoyed a warm and kind relationship with the director of the school, Stanisław Dąbrowski, and many of the professors and instructors, who included both Poles and some Germans. They devoted themselves to teaching us everything they knew, and always treated us respectfully, as future professionals and peers. They made no distinction between Christians and Jews. Everything I acquired during those years—the discipline, the technical knowledge, the refinement of my talent—helped me survive later on.

My relationships with my classmates were cordial, although we never mixed socially outside school. However, the general anti-Semitic atmosphere did occasionally influence them. I experienced two incidents of overt anti-Semitism during my years at the school. The first one happened shortly after I had started school in 1936. One day, I was sitting in class, drawing a piece of sculpture, mastering the definition of light and shadow. Suddenly a fellow student, Jan Jarząb, sitting right behind me, hit me sharply in my back. "*Parszywy Żydzie!*" (Rotten Jew!) he said. Then he insulted my mother. I was no stranger to the vernacular, so I responded in kind. He hit me again. My teacher, Professor Aleksander Sołtan, demanded to know what was going on. I didn't say anything. But Jarząb said, "We don't need Jews in this school. Get out and go to Palestine!"

Professor Sołtan came to my defense. He denounced the attack and the attacker in no uncertain terms. Violence between students in the class was unacceptable, he said. He reminded us that we were living in very sad times and would have enough trouble dealing with our enemies. We had to stick together. I heard angry mutterings from some of my classmates, calling him *żydowski pachołek* (Jewish lackey).

At the end of the day, another professor, Bolesław Penciak, escorted me home to prevent any further attacks by this same student, who had threatened to finish me after school. Later, my mother and I met with the director of the school, Dąbrowski, to discuss this incident. He also denounced it, although he said that he would not take immediate steps to rectify the situation, for fear of reprisals. However, several months later, this student was expelled. Which means that, on balance, there was more justice than anti-Semitism in the school.

The second anti-Semitic incident involving me took place in 1938 in the school laboratory. A senior named Antoni Cetnarowski, who later became a noted poster designer, cursed me furiously and hit me hard in the stomach. He said that, as a Jew, I did not belong in the school.

21

One other incident occurred that year: my classmate Itzchak Kornblum was beaten and about to be thrown over the stone school wall. Professor Penciak came to his rescue as well.

That same year, 1938, I won first prize in a national poster contest for the Polish Army. My winning entry was a propaganda poster urging people to be thrifty and work hard in order to strengthen the nation. The prize was seventy-five zlotys, a sizeable amount in those days. I donated one-third of the money to the needy, one-third to the Polish Red Cross, and kept one-third for myself.

By the time I was graduated from the Piłsudski School in 1939, the general situation in Poland was very bad. It was a difficult time with a sense of foreboding. War with Germany was in the air. During the summer following graduation, my senior class was sent to a base near the Baltic Sea for two weeks of military training. This had always been compulsory for high school students, but it now took on new importance in light of current events.

We worried about the possibility of German occupation and what that would mean for Poland, and for us as Jews. Old-timers spoke of their experiences during the German occupation in World War I and concluded that we did not need to worry too much. Yet we heard frightening stories about what was happening to Jews in Germany. A relative of my father's, a woman in her late thirties with a young son, visited us in 1938, after having been deported to Poland from Berlin, and described conditions in Germany. We saw disaster approaching but could do nothing about it. We were helpless. We lived locked into an environment from which we couldn't escape. We could only try to make the best of it.

In the meantime, the economic situation in our home was growing worse. Many of my father's instruments were

Author's school photo, 1938

rented or bought on installment. The musicians he dealt with began to disappear and my father could not collect anything from them. (On several occasions, my father simply lent out or even gave instruments away to struggling musicians out of sympathy and pity.)

As the oldest child in the family, nineteen years old in the summer of 1939 (my sister was seventeen, my brothers, fourteen and twelve), I knew I had to help my family. I continued repairing musical instruments at home, but I also had to find a job. Given my interest in graphic design and related techniques, I would have loved to work at the Polish Bureau of Engraving, a state institution. But a Jew would never be hired in a place like that, so this was an empty dream. In those days, there were a number of Jewish printing and lithography shops. Lewin-Epstein, one of the leading printers of the Talmud and other religious Jewish books in Warsaw, was just down the street from my home, at 38 Pawia Street. I tried to get a job there but I was still a beginner, and jobs were hard to find with the threat of war hanging overhead. In the meantime, I did odd jobs in a lithographic shop where a friend and fellow graduate of the Piłsudski School, Izak Rubin, was employed. Izak was very devoted to me and helped me whenever he could. He knew that our situation was quite serious.

And so the depressing summer of 1939 moved to its climax.

3

At about five o'clock on Friday morning, September 1, 1939, we were awakened by pounding on the door. From the street we heard sounds of running, crying, quite a commotion. My aunt Bela, my mother's youngest sister, was at the door to tell us that war had broken out. She was crying. My mother was crying. There was tremendous anxiety. Where will we go? How will we get food? How will we get money? What will happen now?

People were streaming out of their houses into the streets. We tried to listen to the news on our small crystal radio but the sounds from *Hoycher Moyshe,* Tall Moshe's candy store across the street drowned out the earphones. He had turned the loudspeaker of his store radio toward the street so we could all hear Polish Radio announce that war had broken out and mobilization was under way. Certain age groups were told to report immediately for military duty. A few hours later, posters with the same information appeared. I wasn't afraid of being drafted because I was only nineteen and the draft started at twenty-one. My father also could not be drafted because, at fifty-four, he was too old. We were, however, very concerned about my mother's five brothers still in Poland who were of mobilization age.

Groups of people banded together in the courtyards of their buildings, frantically debating: Where to go? What to do? But there wasn't much time for discussion, because within a few hours, the Germans started bombing the city.

Warsaw was bombed continuously during the first weeks of the war. The few Polish planes that responded to the German raids during the early hours of the war were quickly silenced. The air raids lasted anywhere from ten minutes to half an hour without letup. The German planes came in packs, dozens of planes at a time. First came the Stukas, light attack planes, dropping *feuerbomben*, phosphorus bombs. Phosphorus burns through everything, melts everything it touches. The houses were built out of brick and wood and they burned easily. Then the heavier, four-engine Heinkels followed, dropping regular explosive bombs that just ripped the buildings apart.

There was panic. People didn't know what to do. Everywhere you saw people running, carrying heavy bundles. Pillows, blankets, some clothes, whatever you could grab. You were running for your life. You were afraid that the fire would burn you, that you might be hit. The planes were coming from all over. I saw the bombs falling, zigzagging through the air like a beautiful game of little flies and little birds, and sowing death. (Years later, in 1945, the Allies carried out the same kind of bombing against the Germans at Dresden. I experienced that bombing. I lived to see the Germans go through what we went through during those first few weeks of the war.)

My family ran, too. We picked up our pillows, threw a few pieces of clothing over our arms and ran like crazy ones to my aunt Pesa, my mother's younger sister, and her husband, my uncle Avraham Mendel Drajer, who lived with their son Moshe on Dzielna Street, one block away from us. Their apartment was right across from the Saint Augustine Church. We thought it would be safer there because surely the Germans would respect the sanctity of a church and not bomb it. (And in fact, the church did survive the war. It witnessed the destruction of the entire Jewish ghetto, and the destruction of Warsaw in the 1944 Polish uprising. Though badly damaged during the war, it remained standing.)

Toward the late afternoon, we came back to our own apartment and decided to stay there. Whenever the sirens announced another air raid, we would rush down to the basement of our building. (Most buildings in Warsaw had cellars into which people crowded.) The building was owned by three Jewish partners, Ber, Kirszencweig, and Wajnberg. Wajnberg lived just below us on the second floor with his three sons and two daughters. (When the ghetto was later established, one of his sons became a Jewish policeman and played a very ugly role in my mother's deportation in 1942.) Sometime during those first weeks of the war, we set up a prayer room in the Wajnberg apartment. We thought we would be safer on a lower floor if a bomb hit the building. But, two weeks later on Rosh Hashanah, when the Germans targeted the Jewish sector with particularly heavy bombing, we had to stop praying there as well and run down to the cellar.

During those first days of the war, the city established air-raid wardens to help evacuate people from buildings hit during the raids and to offer whatever assistance was possible. A call also went out for volunteers to dig anti-tank ditches on the outskirts of Warsaw. I joined thousands of people, Jews and Poles alike, who responded to this call. All these efforts were noble, but hopeless. There was not much anyone could do to hold off the enemy.

The Germans bombed by day, and left the city to burn at night. Fires spread quickly from building to building, so that certain parts of the city were quite badly damaged. There were tremendous flames at night, huge pillars of fire and smoke that hung over the city for weeks, until the capitulation. The fire department was helpless. It couldn't fight the fires because the water filter system broke down and there was no water in the pipes. The building next to ours, Pawia 46, caught fire, but luckily the tenants were able to put it out themselves with water they had stored in their apartments in pails and pots.

Very soon after the outbreak of the war, food shortages developed. Those who had money, ate, those who didn't— like my family—struggled. There were no public kitchens during the fighting because there was no time to organize anything like that. Stores were locked, and people who owned them grabbed the food for themselves. People panicked and started breaking into food warehouses and factories. I remember people running out of one of these warehouses, carrying big metal jars of sour pickles. My uncle Itzchak (who had taught me Hebrew calligraphy) and I even brought home some cans of pickles that looters had dropped in the streets. People also broke into deserted apartments in bombed-out buildings and took whatever food they could carry.

My family had not managed to stock up on food. We had very little storage, and no refrigeration, so we just had some bread and some sugar on hand. We also had very little money. The small amount we had saved in the bank was gone. There was such chaos: the army collapsed, the government disappeared, and the banks shut down. We were left with whatever we had in our pockets, maybe seven zlotys. We survived the first few weeks of the war thanks to the generosity of my aunt Pesa, who was somewhat well off. Her husband, Avraham Mendel, was a meat supplier with major accounts at prisons and military hospitals. He continued to work with his suppliers throughout the German attack and into the German occupation of the city, obtaining meat from smugglers who brought it into the Jewish sector. My aunt and uncle's food storage cellar was well stocked during the early days of the war, and they insisted on sharing their food with us.

For the most part, as I think back to the period between the outbreak of the war and the entry of the Germans into Warsaw, I remember the cooperation among the people in my neighborhood. People cooked together and shared their food. We too sometimes ate with neighbors who had some food to spare.

When the British and the French entered the war a few days later, we thought it would be over very quickly. The happiness of the population was beyond description. But as the days passed, we came to realize that there would be no quick end to the war.

As they drew nearer, the Germans continued to bombard the city from the air and shelled us with heavy artillery on the ground. The hospitals were full of the wounded. The streets were full of corpses. Backyards and courtyards of buildings were turned into temporary graveyards. Dead horses were quickly cut up into meat by the hungry population. There was not a pigeon to be seen; they had all been caught and killed for food.

Sections of the city were isolated from each other because there was neither public transportation nor electricity. There was no water because water tanks and filters were destroyed during the bombing. People drew water from wells dug in the cemeteries.

There was terrible panic. People were running in all directions. Some believed that they could survive better in the countryside where food was more readily available. Men were fleeing because there was an alarm that they, in particular, would suffer if captured by the Germans. The Germans took advantage of this exodus to the villages and outlying areas to strafe the fleeing civilians.

Poland had been divided into the German and Russian zones of occupation by the Hitler-Stalin Pact of 1939. The Bug River, which separated the two zones, was about a six-hour train ride from Warsaw or three days on foot. At this point it was still not that difficult to cross the river. The Germans seemed not to mind and the Russians did not stop anyone from crossing either.

Thousands of people, including several Jews from our building, jammed the highways going east, toward the Soviet zone of occupation and the supposed safety of Russia. Others, including Jews, moved west, leaving the Russian zone for the German-occupied part of Poland. They believed German promises that things would soon be normalized in their part of Poland. Some were returning to relatives left behind in the German zone because they feared that otherwise they would not be reunited. Others became frightened when they learned that a number of Jews were being shipped into the interior of the Soviet Union. (As things turned out, of course, many of these Jews survived the war because, when the Germans attacked the Soviet Union in June, 1941, they were safe in the interior of the Soviet Union.)

Some of my mother's brothers left for Russia. Some turned back later, but my uncle Itzchak, the calligrapher, his wife Malka, and their two children, Moshe and David, continued on into the Soviet Union in November 1939. (We heard from them only once; they had reached the Crimea safely. After that, there was silence. Years later, a Russian officer who liberated me told me that when the Germans conquered the Crimea, they massacred all the Jews. "There are no Jews left in the Crimea," he told me.)

People advised us to leave too, but we never did. We had no money. We had no place to go, no one in any villages to run to. In addition, although my father was influenced by socialist ideas, he did not altogether trust the Soviet Union. The memory of Russian pogroms was too strong. (The nickname among Jews for the Russian, going back to the days of the tsar, was *Fonie ganef*—a thief.) Finally, although people tried to convince me to run away with them, I would not leave my parents, and they did not believe things would get so bad that they should run away. They trusted their memories of the way the Germans had behaved during World War I. Back then, the Germans were considered a better occupier than the tsar, who was no hero to the Jews. The Jews had gotten along with the Germans, could communicate with them because Yiddish was similar to German. (My father, for example, knew German. In fact, our copy of Graetz's "History of the Jews" was in the original German.) Jews had served in the German army and some had even been decorated for bravery. (One of them was hanged in the concentration camp Budzyń later. It was too much for the Germans to tolerate a Jewish lieutenant in their army.) So, all things considered, my father believed that, in the worst case, we would get ration cards and have to do forced labor.

German armored units rolled into Warsaw on September 24, 1939. I saw no fighting in the city. The German units just appeared. Soon, trucks with loudspeakers began to circulate, ordering the population to turn in their weapons. Then posters in German and Polish signed by the German Commandant of Warsaw appeared with the same message. I had a gun that had been left with me by a friend who went to the Soviet Union. I threw it away because I knew if the Germans caught me with it, I'd be in trouble.

During those few weeks between the outbreak of the war and the start of the German occupation of Warsaw, I had not experienced or heard about any overt manifestations of anti-Semitism by the Poles. The shock and panic had been too great for anything like that; all of us, Poles and Jews alike, were facing a common enemy. But as soon as the Germans arrived, anti-Semitism surfaced.

When the Germans moved into the city, they rolled in trucks with bread and soup in order to calm the population and to gain control over it. They ordered that Jews be removed from the lines that immediately formed for the food. Because the Germans could not always distinguish Jews from Poles, they insisted that the Poles eliminate the Jews from the food lines. That way, from the beginning, they separated the population into two camps, the Poles and the Jews. Because the hunger was so great, it was not difficult to get Poles— particularly lower-class elements—to kick Jews off the lines, leaving more food for them. After a while, Jews were afraid even to get on these lines. But the distribution of food did not last very long: the Germans brought in film crews to record the food distribution for propaganda purposes. Once they had finished filming, they stopped giving out food.

One of the first things the Germans did upon entering Warsaw was set up the *Judenrat*, the Jewish Council. The *Juden-*

rat was responsible for carrying out all German decrees. It had to provide Jewish workers for German military units stationed throughout Warsaw and its vicinity. It was ordered to organize work brigades to clean up the damage in the streets, the bombed-out houses, the ruined pavements. Poles who worked in these brigades were treated as paid laborers. Jews, however, were rounded up on the street and forced to work. Stories began to circulate that some Jews had been badly beaten while doing forced labor. Or that the Germans sometimes took down a Jew's address and told him that if he did not report for work the next day, he and his family would be shot. We heard that some Jewish women who had been captured on the street were forced to clean toilets with their underwear and were then forced to put the filthy underwear back on and go home.

My first encounter with a uniformed German took place several days after the beginning of the occupation. I left my home early in the morning heading for the Marshal Piłsudski School. I was going to see the director of my school, Stanisław Dąbrowski. During my school years, he had lashed out at anti-Semitic incidents as being counter to the ethical and democratic principles of the school. I hoped that he could do something for me to help me survive. My parents were very apprehensive about my being in the streets. But I was wearing my school cap with its insignia and I thought students would be safe.

As I walked through the streets not far from school, I noticed a large truck parked with its back lowered. Inside, a number of Jews were sitting, guarded by a German soldier who stood nearby with a rifle. Before I could do anything, another soldier came up to me and asked: "Jude?" (Are you a Jew?) Maybe I could have lied my way out of this situation, particularly because I was wearing my Polish school cap. But I did not. I was too frightened. I said: "I am a Jew." The soldier ordered me to climb into the truck with the others.

There were about ten or twelve Jews in the truck when I first got on. They were fairly young, the oldest was about forty. I asked, "What's going on?" Someone answered, "Don't be scared. They are taking us to work." They were trying to find as favorable an interpretation as possible of the situation they were in. I knew there would be panic in my house because they were expecting my return in about an hour.

After they had collected about forty Jews, two soldiers with guns got into the truck, closed the back and we started to move. Someone asked the soldiers where we were going, and one of them answered: "Don't be afraid, you are going to work." We rode for about thirty minutes. They drove us to a northwest section of Warsaw, a completely non-Jewish area of the city called *Bielany,* where the *Centralny Instytut Wychowania Fizycznego* (Central Institute of Physical Training) stood. We drove into a compound that the Germans had turned into a military area. Everywhere there were signs in German Gothic script. It occurred to me that I could be useful to the Germans as a graphic artist, because I knew Gothic script and could make such signs.

They lined us up in front of the main building. A number of officers came out. The soldier escorting us reported that he was delivering a certain number of Jews to work. Another soldier, wearing the light-colored linen overalls of a work detail, divided us into four groups. He said that we would be working that day repairing water pipes, digging ditches, and asked how many of us knew anything about plumbing. To me the Jews looked like anything but plumbers but suddenly the majority of the Jews claimed they were expert plumbers and other technicians. Then he came over to me and asked what my occupation was. I said that I was a graphic artist. He called over to another soldier standing nearby, "Look at this, here is a *Jude,* a Jew who says he is an artist." This seemed too much for him to digest. Jews had to know their place. He turned to me and said: "You'll be doing some artwork today."

He led me and a group of Jews into a nearby building. He told us to take off our underwear. Then he ordered us to use it to clean the toilets.

Around noon, the German supervisor came out and told us that we would get something to eat once the soldiers had finished their lunch. After a while, they called us over to a field kitchen and poured their leftovers into the pails we had just been using for the clean-up. (They allowed us to rinse them out first.) We passed around the few pails and drank the contents. It consisted of soup with some vegetables floating in it. Some of the Jews asked for cigarettes but the soldiers said they had very few themselves and could not give us any. We got half an hour to eat and rest and then were ordered to come back for more work.

We were constantly told to work faster. The word they used was *tempo,* a word I was to hear many times over the next few years. The day went by with no beatings. They yelled at us and insulted us and cursed us and scared us but there were no beatings.

Several Poles were working at a different part of the compound. I asked one of them, "What's going on here?" He told me that they were employed by the hour and finished at five in the afternoon. But he thought that the Jewish workers might be kept overnight, or longer.

Sure enough, at five o'clock, I saw the Poles leaving the area. Some showed their passes to the guard, others did not. When I saw a group of Polish male and female workers preparing to leave, I walked over to one of the women and told her that I had been captured that day because they had mistaken me for a Jew. My Piłsudski school cap and Warsaw slang must have convinced her, because she told me to walk alongside her. As we passed the guard, some of the Poles held up their passes, and some did not. I made a quick motion toward the guard with my palm and kept moving. Once we were outside, the Polish woman said to me: "Now that you are out, run like hell because I know that you are a Jew." I realized that she had known who I was all along and yet she still helped me.

Now that I had escaped, I had to get home. The trolleys were not running and I had no money. It had taken thirty minutes to get to this place by truck so on foot it would take several hours. I had no choice, so I started to march. From time to time, I saw German patrols but managed to evade them.

(I later learned that the other Jews in my work group were let go after two days of work. The Germans simply picked up a fresh group of Jews who were not exhausted and were therefore better workers. I don't think they ever noticed my disappearance because nobody was punished. This place, *Bielany*, later became a place of torture for Jews.)

When I finally arrived home at about the start of curfew at nine o'clock, I found my family frantic. They embraced me and kissed me despite the stink I brought into the house from my work in the latrines. I tried to tell them how this incident had affected me, that, for the first time, I understood the seriousness of the situation in which we found ourselves. It was not comparable to World War I. These were not the same Germans. What scared me most was their attitude. They acted as though they were the masters of life and death. Their self-assurance was unlimited and you could not communicate with them because they thought of themselves as superior to everyone who was not German. In this brief experience, I had become aware of the difference between the treatment meted out to Jews and to Poles. Poles were treated as workers. Jews were treated as slaves. Jews were animals.

My father disagreed with me. He had always believed in a world where labor and decency would win, and he continued to believe this. He said that the worst that could happen to us was that they would put us to work. I told him he was wrong. He replied that I had run into a bad situation but this was not typical. But my instincts told me that our situation was unusual, scary, and that things would get much worse.

From that time on, I was in despair. I can't say that I grasped that the Germans were out to kill all the Jews. That realization came later, too late. But I knew that we were in for a very difficult time. Our only hope was that the Allies would win the war quickly.

A week later, it was my father's turn to experience what German rule was all about. He and I went to visit a colleague of his, a cellist by the name of Debernitz who was a *Volksdeutscher*, a Pole of German origin. Before the war, I had often picked up the bow of his cello for repair and he would give me a tip of a zloty or two. We decided to visit Debernitz in order to get some advice from him regarding some work for my father or me. I had hoped, for example, to get a job in the graphic arts department of the *Judenrat*, which printed the decrees that the Germans were constantly issuing. Two of my friends, Amram Warszawski and Zosia Rosenstrauch, worked there. Amram had been a classmate of mine in the Piłsudski School and Zosia had studied architecture at the Warsaw Politechnic. I did not have the right influence to get such a job. I thought that maybe, as a *Volksdeutscher*, Debernitz might be able to pull strings there on my behalf.

Debernitz said that he thought things would get better.

He said that once things settled down, they would undoubtedly organize some musical groups and then my father could find work. The situation was difficult for everybody, not just for Jews. He would let us know if he heard of anything. Indeed, he went to intervene on my behalf at the labor department of the *Judenrat,* headed by a Mr. Rozen. Rozen promised to do something for me but I never heard from him after that.

On that visit to Debernitz, my father wore a cap. Normally he wore a hat, but under the occupation he did not want to appear too fancy and he thought that by wearing a cap he would stand out less. We had just left Debernitz's building and were walking up the street when two German soldiers walked up to my father and asked: "Are you Jews?" When my father replied in the affirmative, one of them said: "Jew swine, take your cap off and get off the sidewalk." Before my father could react, the German pulled off his cap, ripping out a handful of hair along with it. My father's head started bleeding. The other soldier threw me against the wall. Then the two of them walked away laughing.

My father was horrified. He said to me: "Motl (his nickname for me), we are lost." When we arrived home, my mother was shocked. She put compresses on my father's head and he went to bed.

When this incident happened, Poles who were nearby reacted rather sympathetically toward us. I could see pity in their faces. They saw our fear but they quickly took off so as not to get involved.

I could understand strangers not wanting to get involved or help us when they saw us being brutalized by the enemy. They were afraid for themselves. But I hoped that people I knew or had studied with might suggest ways to help me and my family survive. I decided to try once again to meet with the director of my school, Stanisław Dąbrowski.

Dąbrowski met me at the doorway of the building and barred me from entering. He told me that, according to German regulations, no Jew was allowed to enter the school. I asked him what I could do, what advice he could give me. He told me: "*Wziąć nóz do ręki, uciec do lasu i bić wroga.*" (Take a knife in your hand, run to the forest, and fight the enemy.)

I was devastated.

4

Shortly after the incident with Dąbrowski, on the advice of my parents, I decided to try to visit my former teacher from the graphics school, Professor Bolesław Penciak. Penciak, a Pole and a graduate of the *Kunstgewerbe Schule* (the School of Applied Arts) in Vienna, was an expert in German calligraphy. I hoped he could help me perfect my skill in this area. In contrast to Dąbrowski, Penciak received me very warmly in his home and spent several hours giving me detailed instruction in Gothic calligraphy. His help improved my skills and gave me greater confidence in my abilities. I will always be grateful to him for his humanity.

Our building, at 48 Pawia Street, was occupied by workers, small businessmen and professionals: artisans, teachers, musicians, a scribe. Every day, a group of people from the building would report to the *Judenrat* office at 26 Grzybowska Street. The *Judenrat* demanded a quota of workers from each building, and also sometimes ordered specific persons to report for work. People reported voluntarily as word had spread that this was the only way to avoid being pressed into forced labor in random street roundups called *łapanki*. Frequently, wealthier Jews paid poor Jews to go to work on their behalf. My brother Pesach and I went there as well, to avoid being rounded up in the street or pulled from our homes. We were assigned to a unit cleaning the debris left in the burned-out buildings. Part of this job involved collecting any pieces of metal—including breaking away the iron balconies—that the Germans could utilize in their war machine. Our group was supervised by my friend Henryk Świętosławski. It was dangerous work and we tried to get out of it, but it was not easy to do so. Besides, at that time, we were "earning" three zlotys and 20 groszy a day for our labor, paid by the *Judenrat*. These few pennies meant a lot to us. They were enough to buy a half loaf of bread. But after a few weeks, payment was stopped. The *Judenrat* said they had no more money.

One day, about the middle of November, 1939, a neighbor of ours, Berl Sztyleryt, a man in his twenties, came to see me and my parents and suggested that I report to the *Judenrat* with him the following morning for a new work assignment. Berl knew that we were hungry and needed help. He advised me to dress deliberately like a poor worker rather than try to look my best because the Germans often beat better-dressed Jews.

The next morning, we reported to the *Judenrat* with several hundred other Jews. We were broken down into work details called companies, of about one hundred each. My company was headed by Aaron Eisenberg, a Jew from Kutno in Pomerania and a teacher by profession. Our destination was Okęcie, the Warsaw airport, which was about nine kilometers from the Jewish part of the city.

We traveled by trolley and on foot, guarded by *Luftwaffe* soldiers. We were among about two thousand Jews reporting for work at the airfield that morning. The Jew in charge of each company delivered his group to the Germans who assigned them to various tasks. I was in a group of fifteen Jews assigned to the *Fahrkolonne*. This was the "Horse and Wagon Unit," a unit of about sixty soldiers and a number of horses and wagons, which was responsible for transporting goods within the airport and its vicinity. The unit was stationed on an old estate, which had stables for the horses.

The Jews in my group were skilled laborers: tailors, shoemakers, saddle makers. Some worked in the kitchen. The German in charge of us asked me what kind of work I did. I said that I was a graphic artist and that I knew Gothic script. He seemed to find this hard to believe, even though Eisenberg had apparently told him earlier that one of the Jews he was delivering that morning was an artist. He said that we would soon find out whether a Jew could do this kind of work.

This man was *Unteroffizier* Willi Pommerenke from Stettin. He was twenty-two years old and had been a student before the war. Pommerenke reported to his superior, Lieutenant Freiherr von Buseck, a man of about forty, fat, with a face like a pumpkin, and a pince-nez sitting on the tip of his nose. He seemed to find everything funny; he kept laughing. Pommerenke reported to Buseck that he had a certain number of Jews and then assigned them to various tasks for the day: so many to the kitchen, so many to the stable, and so on. After all the others had been put to work, Pommerenke marched me to an office and asked what supplies I needed. I replied that I needed a pen, ink, and paper. These were produced immediately.

He then pulled out a big sheet of paper with a large bull's eye on it, a target for shooting. I became frightened: I could imagine him making me hold the target and shooting at it while I held it. He noticed my reaction and told me not to worry. He gave me a typewritten list of the names of the soldiers in the unit and ordered me to write nameplates for them in Gothic script on the back of the big sheet.

I did not have the right pen for this job, because he had given me a pen with a regular point and for calligraphy I needed one with a flat point. I had to improvise. I asked him for a knife. (It was strictly forbidden for a Jew to carry anything of the sort on his person.) He produced a pocketknife and watched me like a hawk to see what I did with it. I sharpened a stick to get the necessary edge and went to work. He was satisfied and left me to work, saying that he would be back shortly. After a while he returned, looked over what I was doing and told me to continue. A short while later he returned again and told me to follow him to his office. There, he asked me what my name was. I told him it was Moses. He said that from now on my name would be *Maxie der Kunstmahler*, the artist. He then showed my work to Buseck.

Buseck liked what I had done and asked me where I had studied. I replied that I had studied at the School of Graphic Arts in Warsaw. He asked where I lived and what my father did. This interrogation took place while Pommerenke stood at attention. Buseck then dismissed us and Pommerenke told me to finish the job. I wrote each name three times, preparing one nameplate for the bed, one for the closet, and one for the trunk of each soldier. I was working at a table in a room with three beds that belonged to soldiers of the unit. Pommerenke told me that I had to clear out of there by noon because the soldiers would be coming back for lunch and I was not to be there when they returned.

He asked me how I was returning home. I told him that I had to wait to be marched back to the Jewish quarter with the rest of the workers at the end of the day. He handed me a package and ordered me to go home now, before noon, and to report to him again the following day. I left by the front gate. The guard challenged me, asking me where I thought I was going. I told him Pommerenke had ordered me to go home, and he let me pass.

I was very curious about what was in the package and opened it as I walked. It contained a large loaf of bread and a package of cheese. I walked home very fast. It took me about an hour. My family was amazed to see me return home so early. They were even more amazed when I showed them the bread and the cheese.

Giving me the food was Pommerenke's own idea. He came from a wealthy family that was in the lumber and ship-building business. Later, Pommerenke told me that his grandfather had blessed him before he left for the war and told him not to mistreat people with whom he came in contact. He said he was sticking to these principles and was not going to mistreat anybody. He showed me a golden pocket watch that he wore around his neck on a chain. His grandfather had given it to him. He thought of this as a talisman that would protect him from harm during the war.

Several days later, he asked me whether I could paint portraits. I said yes because I had learned never to say that there was something I could not do. I knew that he would not sit for the portrait and I would have to work from photographs. He gave me a passport-sized photograph of himself with a tooth missing and told me to paint a portrait of him, with the tooth restored, from the photograph. I was to report to the airfield every morning but he would then send me home to work on the painting there. He gave me a special pass that entitled me to walk home unescorted. It was a white rectangular card, about six by eight inches, with a half-inch green stripe running diagonally across it. Under a photograph of me in the upper left-hand corner, it said, "The Jew shown in this photograph, *Moses Wischogrod* (the German spelling of my name) is permitted to walk unescorted between the airfield and the Jewish district." And underneath, in the left-hand corner: "The authorities are requested to give him every possible assistance in case of need." It was signed and sealed by *Oberst* (Colonel) Vickum, *Kommandant*, *Fliegerhorst* (airport), Okęcie, Warsaw.

He asked me how long it would take me to do the portrait. I told him it would take about two weeks. I made the time last as long as possible because the alternative, the regular slave labor being done at the airport, was hard and dangerous.

The former civilian airport had been turned into a German military airfield. Planes, Stukas and Heinkels, were taking off and landing all the time. There were large camouflaged pits all over the airfield containing bombs, or drums of gasoline. Jews worked everywhere, covering these pits with nets, painting trucks in camouflage colors, cleaning everything, even delivering bombs, though we were never allowed to approach the planes. Many Jews working at the airfield ended up with broken arms or legs or other injuries. Some resulted from accidents. Others came from being driven like animals, beaten with whips or pipes.

Compared to these conditions, the fifteen of us assigned to the *Fahrkolonne* were treated rather well. We came in direct contact with the soldiers and officers of this unit. We fixed their jackets, washed their clothes, cleaned their rooms. While a distance obviously remained between them and us, some human relationships were established. Every once in a while, they would throw a slice of bread or a couple of cigarettes our way. *Unteroffizier* Otto Fischer of the *Fahrkolonne*, for example, was considered a "good German." In our prisoners' lexicon, this meant a German who did not beat us. He limited his cruelty to sarcastic anti-Semitic remarks. He blamed the Jews for the war and cursed us.

Another advantage of this unit was that much of the work was done indoors so if it rained or was cold, we had somewhere to go to dry out or warm up. This was a lifesaver, because most of us were poorly dressed. This had to do with the kind of work we were doing, which was physical, difficult, and dirty. But in addition, we were safer if we dressed in shabby clothes; the Germans were less offended by Jews who looked poor and miserable, and were therefore less likely to strike out at us.

The Jews in my group were, of course, aware that I only reported for work in the morning and then went right home. But they did not mind because they considered me a loyal friend. In addition, my talent established a somewhat warmer relationship between the Germans and us and this was to everyone's advantage.

I knew that my soft job would not last long, that my relationship with Pommerenke was too good to be true. I dragged out the painting job for the two weeks we had agreed upon, which was as long as I dared. During that time, he frequently gave me food, telling me to hide it. When he could not give me anything, he apologized, saying that there was a shortage of bread that day and therefore he could not take any of it. On a number of occasions, he told me that if I waited until 2:30 P.M., when they distributed the leftovers from the soldiers' lunch, I could get some. But I was afraid to wait because if I were seen hanging around without working, I might be assigned to some other work detail and I wanted to avoid that.

Finally, I delivered the portrait, drawn in black charcoal.

He liked it very much and thanked me. Then he asked me how much he owed me for it. The question came as a total shock. There was something human about that man. I told Pommerenke that he owed me nothing because I was simply afraid to ask him for money. He handed me twenty German marks, saying that this was for retouching his tooth in the portrait. I thanked him but gave him back the money. I was afraid to take it because it was forbidden for a Jew to hold German money.

Around this time, an *Unteroffizier* Sasse appeared. He had been an assistant to the blacksmith. He quickly came to the conclusion that the Jews working for the *Fahrkolonne* had it too good and this was particularly true of me. Somehow, I knew instinctively that he would not like me. I was afraid of any changes. Sure enough, soon Pommerenke disappeared. I could not, of course, ask the Germans what had happened to him, but Eisenberg, in charge of all the Jewish workers, found out that he had been transferred.

I did my best to avoid Sasse, but he caught up with me one morning. He surprised me with a powerful kick into my lower spine that hurt me badly. Maybe he was jealous that I had done a portrait for Pommerenke, although he claimed that he wouldn't ever like to have a portrait from a "*Schwein Jude,*" a Jewish pig. I never did any art for him. Soon afterward, he disappeared from the unit and I never saw him again.

5

With Pommerenke gone, there was no further need for the *Kunstmahler* in the *Fahrkolonne*. Eisenberg assigned me to a regular work unit that unloaded coal from railroad cars. Some of the workers stood on the open railroad cars throwing chunks of coal onto the ground. Other Jews picked it up and moved it to its destination. With three or four Jews working, it took approximately one to two hours to unload a car. At times they would reduce it to two Jews per car. This happened when the coal consisted of smaller pieces. Then the work was easier because we were given shovels. For bigger chunks we used our bare hands.

A redheaded Pole from Silesia, a *Volksdeutscher,* was in charge of this work. In general, the *Volksdeutsche* were considered traitors by the Poles, and were disliked by both Poles and Jews. If you spoke to them in Polish, they pretended not to understand even though, of course, they did. This man, a very rough person, was eager to show his devotion to the Germans by supervising the unloading of as many cars as possible. He had the help of a number of other *Volksdeutsche* who beat Jews in order to make them work faster. I worked at this job for several weeks and it was horrible because we were beaten regularly.

After several weeks, this *Volksdeutscher* approached me and asked what special skills I had. I was amazed that he spoke to me, but it turned out that Eisenberg had told him that he was wasting a great talent. He wanted me to paint a portrait of his girlfriend. Of course, I told him I would do it (as if I had a choice!), but I offered to paint his portrait first. I had learned from my experience that the Germans were vain and liked pictures of themselves showing all their military insignias and proving their superiority. He produced a photograph of himself and told me to work from it.

He took me to a large storage shack. It had a table in it but was very cold and I knew that I would not be able to draw there because my hands would get too stiff. So he asked me where I wanted to work. I said I would prefer to take it home and work there. (I was thinking of Pommerenke who had sent me home early to do his portrait.) He replied that this was not possible because if anybody came around asking for a count of the Jews, I had to be present. In any case, he said, he was doing me enough of a favor by having me paint his picture.

He had me improvise a kind of stove out of a barrel, knocking some holes in its side, putting in some coal and lighting it. I brought some paper and pencils from home and finished his portrait in three days. When it was finished, I gave it to him. He did not thank me or tell me whether he liked it. He never mentioned his girlfriend. I went back to shoveling coal.

Some time later, Eisenberg told me that Pommerenke had reappeared and was asking for me. I soon found myself reassigned to the *Fahrkolonne*. Pommerenke told me he had liked my portrait so much, he had shown it to his friends and now there were several requests for portraits. One of those requests came from the cook of the unit, Alfred. I hoped that if I pleased him I would get food to eat there and some to take home to my family.

Alfred warned me that working for him would not be as pleasant as working for Pommerenke. Pommerenke had all kinds of friends among the brass because he had money to throw around but he, Alfred, was just a simple cook. He told me that I could work in the basement of the canteen while the tables were clear. I had to get out by 12:00 when the soldiers came in for lunch and could resume work at 2:30. He added sarcastically that I could then stick my head in the soup kettle and drown in it, if I wished.

I first did a quick charcoal drawing of him because he told me he might be transferred. He also gave me a photograph of his girlfriend and I drew a portrait of her in charcoal as well. I finished the portraits in a few days and he liked them.

At first Alfred seemed pleasant enough. Then, suddenly, a complete change of attitude came over him. He became very nervous. He gave everyone in the kitchen dirty looks, and kept mumbling to himself. A friend of mine, Mark Mandeltort, later told me that he had heard from an older German blacksmith that members of Alfred's family had been killed in Germany. This probably caused his change of attitude. The brothers Gruszka, two Jews who had been assigned to clean the kitchen, warned me to stay out of his way.

We usually ate only after the soldiers finished their meal. Jews would mill around the entrance to the kitchen, waiting like hungry dogs for their food. We were given whatever was left over in the kettles, with some water added to thin the food stuck to the sides of the pots. On this particular day, I was standing at the back of the group. Alfred spotted me. As soon as he saw me, he called me over, saying that today I would eat myself full. He brought out a pail of hot soup, grabbed me by the hair and stuck my face into the hot soup. He screamed: "Today is the end of soup, the end of all of you Jews. I don't want to see you in the kitchen again." My entire face was burned. I ran away screaming. Most of all, I was afraid that he would run after me and finish me off.

There was nothing I could do about this treatment. Nobody would stand up for a Jew who had been mistreated.

My face was burned but luckily my eyes were not injured. I had to stay home until the burns healed and told Eisenberg that I needed to be excused from the airfield for a few days. This involved considerable hardship at home because I was the only source of food but I simply could not go to work with the shape my face was in. On the other hand, it was vital for me to keep this job. It was the only way I could gain access to the gentile world where I could sell or barter something and bring some food home.

At about this time, my father started to deal in cigarettes. He got tobacco from my mother's brother Velvel who lived at 51 Pawia Street, adjacent to the National Tobacco Company. Poles were apparently stealing tobacco from the warehouse and selling it to Jews, including my uncle who then gave some to my father. My father traded anything he could put his hands on for the tobacco: clothing, sheets, blankets, silverware. We bought cigarette tubes and the whole family began working at home stuffing tobacco into the tubes. My father would then venture out to sell the cigarettes.

He made a good impression on the peasants and they often bought from him.

Doing this was dangerous. On one occasion when he was selling cigarettes at the *Kiercelego* market place, a peasant approached him and told him to be careful, that although he was a good Jew, he should not come out too frequently because someone might do him harm. My father sensed that it was, in fact, *this* peasant who was threatening him. He continued to sell cigarettes, however, and in this way, we managed to scrape by for a little while. Soon, however, the cigarette business stopped altogether. The smugglers who were stealing the tobacco stopped supplying my uncle Velvel. We never found out the reason. In any case, this avenue of survival was now closed. My father went to the *Judenrat* to see whether they had anything for him to do but they did not.

My father became something of a street politician. He was considered particularly well informed. Because he read German, he would interpret the German newspaper *Voelkischer Beobachter* (The National Observer) for us, reading mostly between the lines. I have vivid memories of him standing in the street or the courtyard surrounded by Jews eager to hear his latest analysis. He would analyze the military situation and always come out with an optimistic conclusion. His message was always one of hope, probably the result of wishful thinking. This optimism prevailed, with ups and downs, until the end of 1941, when we were all stricken with typhus. By that time, in spite of his religious faith, hunger and the suffering of the ghetto had broken his spirit.

During this period when I did not go to work at the airfield because of my burned face, I have a particularly sharp recollection of my father. He would get up early in the morning, wrap himself in *tallis* and *tfillin* (phylacteries) and begin his prayers. He prayed for a very long time. Before the war, he prayed quickly because he had things to do. Now he had nowhere to go. The synagogues were not functioning any more and it seemed that the *tallis* also gave him warmth because we had no coal to heat the oven and our apartment was terribly cold.

It was painful to watch my father in a motionless position, deep in thought. All I heard were deep sighs and groaning. I felt the world was coming to an end.

6

After about a week at home, my face was sufficiently healed for me to go back to work at the airport. That's when I got to know a wonderful Jew named Stoliński from the town of Mława. He was the leader of one of the Jewish work units. A man with a rough, square face, he screamed terribly at the workers under him, and this was a very good thing. Screaming was a method used by the Germans to terrify the Jews. When the Germans heard a Jewish foreman screaming, echoing their shouts, using their curses, they were pleased. They would stand by and smile, their whips in their hands, and let the Jew do the screaming. This way the Germans were satisfied and fewer Jews got hurt.

Eisenberg asked Stoliński to take me into a new unit that worked outdoors at various tasks. At that particular time they were working at rolling barrels, metal drums that contained oil and gasoline. These barrels arrived by truck and hundreds of Jews were assigned to roll them to different parts of the airport. After working with the barrels for a while, I was switched to something called the *Fahrbereitschaft,* a motorized unit at the airfield. I became a bootblack and did other personal services for the Germans, such as washing socks and the floors of their rooms. One day, a German soldier, *Obergefreiter* Karl Fischer, asked me whether I could make some signs for him. He had heard about me from Stoliński who, like Eisenberg, was always singing my praises to the Germans, saying how talented I was and that they should use me if they needed anything artistic. He did this not only for me but for many others, like tailors, mechanics, and shoemakers. If he could get any Jew indoors, out of the cold, he was delighted. It was to everybody's advantage for the Germans to think that there were many skills among the Jews. Fischer asked me whether I could make signs in Gothic script and I said yes. He wrote something on a piece of paper and ordered me to make a sign of it in Gothic script. When I read it, I was shocked. It said: "*Für Juden und Hunde Zutritt Verboten!*" (For Jews and dogs entry forbidden!) I knew the order had to be carried out so I did it. When the sign was finished, Fischer placed it on the door of the lavatory used by the German personnel and it remained there for a number of months while I was working there.

At another time, my job was to assist a German in camouflaging vehicles. He gave me a spray gun and told me to spray-paint a truck. After a while, I told him that I needed a mask because the lacquer spray was choking me. He replied: "*Jude-Hund* (You Jew-dog). Protective masks are only *für Deutsche* (for Germans)." If I suffocated, that was fine with him. In the meantime, I should be grateful that I worked indoors, in the hangar. In fact, I should be so grateful that when I reported to work the next day, I should bring him a golden watch. I told him I had no golden watch. He replied that this was my problem, he wanted a golden watch and it was my job to get him one. Stupidly, I asked him how much he wanted to spend on it. (My reaction seems so naïve. Looking back, I realize that this naïveté was the result of terrible fear. My whole experience of going to the airfield was under terror and threat. The only thing that gave me the strength to keep going there was the thought of bringing home a piece of bread. Because at home they were dying. You could almost say I was playing a game of pretending that I was dealing with a normal human being who just wanted a watch. Or maybe I still wanted to believe in the goodness of a human being.) He pulled me behind the truck and kicked me vigorously. This seemed very persuasive to me and I told him I would do my best. He wrote down my address and this scared me. I was afraid he would come looking for me and harm my family.

The next day I returned. I still didn't have a gold watch. My mother suggested I give him an alarm clock that we had at home instead. It was an antique, with delicate engravings. He took the clock, placed it on the pavement, smashed it and kicked me. He told me to get the hell out of there, to go back to my group leader and tell him that he had no use for me. He would find another "Judas" who would give him what he wanted. So I lost my job.

During the periods when we worked at the airport, individuals would sometimes slip away from the marching group on the way to work and disappear into the Aryan sector for several hours to obtain food, money, or whatever. The Jewish group leaders knew this was going on and arranged for them to leave the groups at certain points and rejoin them on the way back from work. The Germans who escorted us could usually be bribed to overlook the disappearance of some Jews for several hours.

One day I also slipped away from the group to visit some of my father's gentile colleagues on the Aryan side. They owed us money for musical instruments they had either bought or rented before the war. My first stop was Wiktor Tychowski, the guitarist. As I moved through the streets of the Aryan sector, I shoved my armband into my pocket.

(We had been wearing armbands since December, 1939. They were white bands, at least ten centimeters wide, with a blue Star of David. They came in two varieties: cloth, made of torn-up sheets, and white cardboard. People produced them at home and sold them on the street. The cardboard ones were cheaper, but couldn't be crumpled up and hidden away quickly, which was especially important if you were venturing into the Aryan sector. My mother made mine, out of some white fabric, and I stenciled on the star.)

Tychowski opened the door. Visiting him at the time was a Polish police sergeant. When Tychowski saw me, he said: "My God, what are you doing here?" Because I was not wearing an armband, the policeman did not realize what was going on until he saw Tychowski's shock and then he immediately understood. As a member of the Polish police, he had sworn an oath of allegiance to the occupying Germans and it was his duty to turn me in. Had he done so, I would probably have been killed. The policeman turned to me and said: "Get the hell out of here before I kill you." I ran down the three or four flights of the building as fast as I could without collecting any of the money Tychowski owed us for a guitar.

I headed for another colleague of my father's, the jazz drummer Zofia Wierchowska who lived on Filtrowa Street. She had often been to our house and had rented a set of drums from us. I went to collect the payment she owed us. She smiled at me. "After the war," she said.

In general, we were taken out to work at the airfield on

Saturdays, but not on Sundays. Sunday was a day of rest. One Saturday, Pommerenke ordered me to meet him instead at three o'clock in the afternoon at 9 Przejazd Street, not far from the Tłomackie Synagogue. This area was on the border between the Jewish and Aryan sectors, but, as the ghetto had not yet been established, there was still free movement between these areas. I was on time, dressed as neatly as possible in the best of my lousy suits, in a shirt that my mother had cleaned and ironed. I had also made sure there were no lice on me. (I used to clean hundreds of lice off my body and my clothing, just sweep them off and throw them into the fire.) At precisely three, Pommerenke arrived in a *doroshka,* a one-horse buggy with a driver. He jumped off gracefully, holding a bouquet of flowers. He was very elegantly dressed in uniform, with white gloves, and he motioned to me with a smile to follow him. I slid off my armband, put it in my pocket, and followed him up to an apartment on the second floor, where I had previously noticed a big European balcony on which there was an assemblage of young people.

There was a cocktail party going on for military personnel of the *Wehrmacht* and the *Luftwaffe,* of all ranks, and a number of civilians. Everyone—but me—was German. There was a highly civilized, cultured atmosphere of bowing and kissing the hand, and drinking and toasting each other and exchanging pleasantries. Everyone was very polite.

Pommerenke motioned to me to come in and feel free. He introduced me to the hostess, a German woman, as the *Kunstmahler.* I greeted everyone with a deep bow, in the respectful, Polish style. Then he called over a young woman in her late twenties, good-looking, blond, with Nordic features. She must have known beforehand that I would be there because she produced a photograph, which she first showed him for his approval. Then he gave it to me, and told me to deliver a nice piece of art for this nice young lady, an enlargement of this photograph. I told him, "Yes, I will do it." He asked if I would like a drink. I didn't feel comfortable drinking with them, or getting involved in any conversations with anyone there; where would they lead? It would come out that I was "a Judas." I assumed that some of them knew who I was, but I didn't know for sure. So I replied, "no, thank you, I am very much in a hurry." I took the photograph, bowed again, and left.

This was a shocking experience for me. Never in my life did I expect to be invited to any type of private party of Germans, military personnel and civilians, in the city of Warsaw.

I came home to a scene of bewilderment: Where have you been? What happened? My parents could hardly believe the story. I told them, "I don't know what's going to happen to me next." I could only hope that as long as I kept doing these assignments for him, I was in so-called good hands, and nothing bad would happen to me. At the same time, I was developing a certain confidence in myself that my work was being accepted and I could do some good for my family.

I worked on the portrait at home for several days and nights. When I finished, I brought it to the airfield and gave it to him.

Around Passover, 1940, an order came to stop the use of Jewish workers at the airport. During this period, thousands of Jews were being herded into Warsaw from the surrounding towns and villages. Hunger and disease had become widespread and the Germans were afraid of being exposed to infectious diseases. From Passover, 1940, until the establishment of the ghetto on November 15, 1940, no Jews were allowed to work at the airport.

Once again, my friend, Izak Rubin, was a lifesaver. He

appeared at my door and suggested that I work for him, designing patterns for use in the lithography shop where he worked. His boss agreed to this arrangement and I started working at home. I created pattern designs—ornaments and flowers—on heavy lithograph stones from which the design was imprinted onto textiles.

This shop was one of many the Germans set up in the Jewish sector to provide them with goods. These later developed into the "protected shops" in the ghetto. People who worked in these shops sometimes got special identity cards that gave them a false sense of security because these cards were supposed to protect the bearer and his family.

After a few months the business collapsed because the Germans simply came and took away the lithograph presses.

One day, I came home to find my father terribly agitated. It was May 10, 1940, and the Germans had just invaded Paris. He told me the following story: Late one night many years earlier, around 1905, my father had been practicing the clarinet when he heard noises outside his door. He went to investigate and found a small, pale boy of about ten years old standing there and listening. My father invited him in to warm up and asked what he was doing out alone so late at night. The boy, whose name was Berele Szersznajder (Bernard Scherschneider), explained that he was helping his family by doing all kinds of errands, including taking out people's garbage, in order to collect some tips. Even by the standards of the struggling working-class Jews of Warsaw, Berele's family was extremely poor. His father was a porter who could barely support his wife and several children. The family lived in a subbasement on Wołynska Street, in the poorest section of the Jewish sector of Warsaw. My father asked him if he liked music. Berele replied that he did, but he would rather learn to be a tailor. My father helped him get a job and become a tailor. Later, he helped him leave Warsaw for Paris, where he eventually became a wealthy dress manufacturer. Now the Germans had invaded Paris. My father cried out, "What will happen to my Berele now?"

Meanwhile, our situation was difficult. My brother Pesach was working, substituting for Jews who were unable or unwilling to work. For this, he usually earned about five zlotys a day, enough to buy a bit of bread or a few saccharine tablets in the Aryan sector. The money he earned was not very much but it helped.

My sister, who was now eighteen, did not work. We were very concerned about her safety and kept her at home. The outside world was simply too dangerous for a young woman. Germans often came into the Jewish sector to have a little fun, and would rape and kill. There were even cases where Jewish policemen would go into an apartment and rape a girl.

Late one night in the summer of 1940, we heard pounding on the main door of our building. Four members of the *Feldpolizei*, military police who patrolled the ghetto after dark, entered our building on the pretext of conducting an inspection. In reality they were looking to rob and have some fun. They entered the apartment of our next-door neighbors, the Szermans. These were the musicians who had joined us frequently for our musical sessions in our apartment. The *Feldpolizei* noticed all their musical instruments and asked the brothers to play for them. In the deadly silence of the night, the sudden sound of jazz made us shiver. Then, for about an hour, we heard terrible screams from all over the building.

In our apartment, we had a storage space near the toilet which we had fixed up as a hiding place. One or two persons could crawl into it and we closed it with a wooden board which was made to look like part of the wall. That night the older of my two brothers, Pesach, and my sister hid in that space because we were afraid that the Germans would visit our apartment as well. Luckily, they left us alone.

We never found out exactly what had happened in the various apartments that night. Husbands and fathers would not talk so we could only use our imagination. All we knew was that eventually, after a couple of hours, they left. They even gave the musicians cigarettes.

At night, we were largely in the dark because there was no electricity. We used carbide lamps that gave off a faint blue light and a very unpleasant smell. Often people did not even get undressed at night because of the constant fear that they might come and get you.

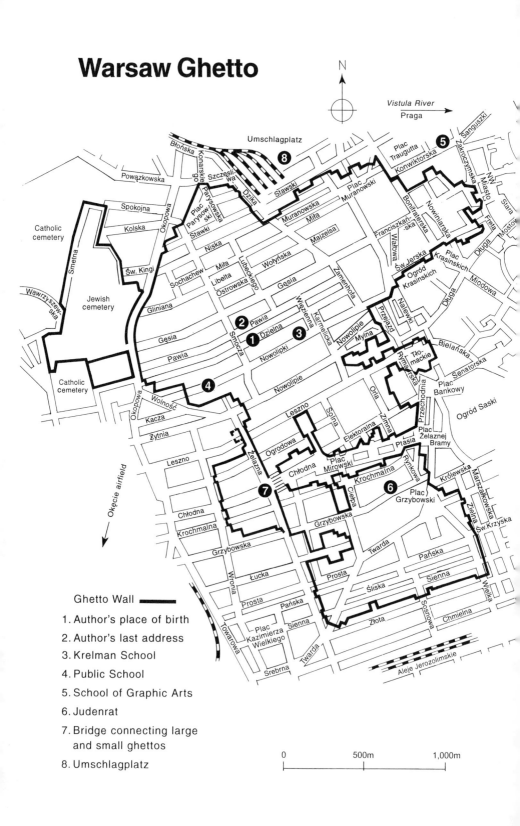

Warsaw Ghetto

N

Vistula River
Praga →

Umschlagplatz

8

5

Błońska
Konarskie-go
Szczęśli-wa
Powązkowska
Dzika
Sławki
Plac Traugutta
Konwiktorska
Sanguszki
Zakroczymska
NW Miasto
Stara

Spokojna
Plac Parysow-ski
Parysowska
Muranowska
Miła
Plac Muranowski
Franciszkań-ska
Bonifraterska
Nowiniarska
Freta
Mostowa
Długa

Catholic cemetery
Kolska
Okopowa
Sławki
Niska
Małzelsa
Wałowa
Długa

Smetna
Sochachew
Miła
Lubeckiego
Wołyńska
Gęsia
Zamenhofa
Św. Jerska
Ogród Krasinskich
Plac Krasinskich
Miodowa

Św. Kingi
Libelta
Ostrowska
Nalewki
Długa

Jewish cemetery
Gliniana
Pawia
Więzienna
Karmelicka
Nowolipie
Przejazd
Bielańska
Senatorska

Wawrzy szew. ska
2 Pawia
1 Dzielna
3
Smocza
Nowolipki
Myjna
Tło-mackie
Rymarska

Gęsia
Pawia
Nowolipie
Orla
Zimna
Przechodnia
Plac Bankowy

Catholic cemetery
4
Okopowa
Wolność
Leszno
Solna
Elektoralna
Plac Żelaznej Bramy
Ogród Saski

Kacza
Żytnia
Ogrodowa
Chłodna
Plac Mirowski
Ptasia

Leszno
Żelazna
Chłodna
Krochmalna
Krochmalna
Rynkowa
Plac Grzybowski
Królewska
Marszałkowska

Okęcie airfield
7
6
Zielna
Św. Krzyska

Chłodna
Krochmalna
Grzybowska
Twarda
Pańska
Sienna
Wielka

Grzybowska
Wronia
Łucka
Prosta
Śliska
Sosnowa
Chmielna

Prosta
Pańska
Sienna
Złota

Towarowa
Plac Kazimierza Wielkiego
Sienna
Twarda
Aleje Jerozolimskie

Srebrna

Ghetto Wall ▬▬▬

1. Author's place of birth
2. Author's last address
3. Krelman School
4. Public School
5. School of Graphic Arts
6. Judenrat
7. Bridge connecting large and small ghettos
8. Umschlagplatz

0   500m   1,000m

7

The Warsaw ghetto was sealed off on Monday, November 15, 1940. Rumors had been circulating for weeks about the establishment of a ghetto. The exchange of populations had been going on for a while. Poles were moved out of the Jewish quarter and Jews were moved in. It was obvious that a ghetto would be established but nobody knew when.

The ghetto did not become reality until five o'clock on the morning of the fifteenth. On that day, Jews still living outside this designated area received urgent orders to move within it. There still was no complete wall around the ghetto, only barbed wire, which was guarded by the Polish police and the Germans. We noticed that brick walls were being erected at certain points, and, within a short time, the entire wall was raised.

The reason the Germans gave for the establishment of the ghetto was that it was necessary to prevent the spread of disease. They posted signs all around the ghetto saying *Seuchensperhgebiet* (Epidemic Quarantine Zone). Jews were forbidden to leave the ghetto and gentiles were forbidden to enter it without a permit. The penalty for violating this order was death. At first, Jews who were moved into the ghetto could bring their furniture and other personal belongings with them but later they were allowed to take with them only what they could carry.

Many Jews felt more secure within the ghetto. Many of them were not from Warsaw proper but from outlying towns and villages around Warsaw with small Jewish populations where they felt much more exposed. Being together with so many other Jews gave them a sense of security. Those who had friends or relatives in the ghetto were, of course, better off. Those who had no one were in a much more difficult position. The *Judenrat* quickly set up shelters in synagogues, warehouses, and schools for those who had no place to stay. The American Jewish Joint Distribution Committee financed much of this activity. Conditions in these places were very bad. People slept on the floor and they could not change their clothes or wash. Sometimes, the *Judenrat* simply ordered private families to take in refugees. Soon after the ghetto was established, we were ordered to give our bedroom to a family from Łódź consisting of a husband, a wife, and a five-year-old boy. After a few months they moved out because they found a larger place. Some months later I saw our former tenant marching with a group of workers. I never saw him again after that. No one else was ever assigned to our apartment.

For my family, the main problem was that I was the main supporter of the family and the possibility of leaving the ghetto was now gone. I had to come up with new ways to keep us going.

Before the establishment of the ghetto, after the work at the airfield stopped, I had established a little calligraphy business. I made "death announcement" posters. The death rate had gone up very sharply and since the ghetto bulletins had stopped appearing, there was no way of announcing deaths. When someone died, posters were put up at the entrance of the house of the deceased and around the neighborhood announcing the death and the time and place of the funeral.

The posters I produced had a black frame which I drew ahead of time. When an order came, I would quickly fill in the details and deliver the posters to the apartment of the deceased or the funeral establishment, a small store with a dozen or so plain pine coffins. In the early days of the ghetto, these establishments were almost always busy, full of families sitting and discussing the burial of a loved one. This was possible only for families that could still afford to give their deceased a decent funeral. The coffin would be brought to the apartment where the *taharah,* the ritual purification of the body, was performed. One of the funeral establishments I worked for was run by the Bieda brothers. I was paid three zlotys for a poster and a family would take one or two. Such posters were a luxury that not everybody could afford. On the black market, a loaf of bread cost about nine or ten zlotys. If I made ten posters a day I could earn 30 zlotys. With that I could buy a loaf of bread, some rice, sugar, soap, or some other things.

At the beginning, the dead were still transported to the cemetery in coffins. Five or six coffins at a time were piled on a handcart, and the relatives of all the deceased walked behind the cart to the cemetery. If the family had a little more money, a black cloth with a Star of David was used to cover the coffin. Funerals usually took place early in the morning or late at night. After a while, two bodies were put into one coffin. At the cemetery, the bodies were taken out of the coffins which were taken back to the ghetto to be reused.

Sometimes, members of the burial units filled the empty coffins with food to be smuggled into the ghetto on the return trip. Occasionally, mock funerals were held in which no bodies were taken out at all, but the coffins were brought back filled with food. This was a dangerous operation and not a few people lost their lives smuggling food into the ghetto. Many persons had to be bribed, including the Polish police and the Germans guarding the ghetto gates. Some Germans could be bribed and others could not. Some accepted bribes and then killed the Jews anyway. You had to know who you were dealing with. In addition, guards were changed frequently and if one was bribed, he could disappear and be replaced by one who was not yet bribed. So you had to be very alert.

As time went on, people no longer conducted funerals in the normal sense of the word. They simply carried the naked corpses out to the street, covered them with some cloth or a newspaper, and left them to be picked up by the burial units assigned by the *Judenrat*. The dead were not put into coffins but simply piled on the hand carts and taken to the cemetery where they were buried in mass graves.

As the situation became more catastrophic, my poster business began to decline and finally collapsed altogether. Fewer people could afford posters. In addition, people began to hide the death of their loved ones in order to use their ration cards to get a little more food.

The ration card was yellow and had the word *Lebensmittelkarte* (ration card) printed on it. It was divided into little squares. Each square had a number and specified bread, sugar, saccharine, honey, or marmalade, all artificial prod-

68

ucts. The distribution of these cards had started before the establishment of the ghetto. Even if you had ration cards, you were not assured of getting food because often the stores simply did not have anything, with or without ration cards. Of course, you also had to pay for the food so that if you had no money, the ration cards were of no use. Sometimes we would hand a storekeeper a coupon for a bread and he would give us half a bread. In effect, we sold him the other half of the ration card instead of paying with money. I had a friend, Yankel Flasterstein, whose father had a little grocery store and he helped us very often. For those who had money, meat, cheese, and butter were smuggled in from the outside. But we could not even dream of such delicacies. Our diet consisted mostly of bread, rotten vegetables, and marmalade. We also occasionally got some chicory, a coffee substitute.

Meanwhile, typhus was spreading wildly. Whole buildings were taken for delousing, in operations conducted jointly by Polish and Jewish police, the *Jüdische Ordnungsdienst*. At five o'clock in the morning, men, women, and children were marched off by force to the delousing stations. All their hair was shaved and they were smeared with a strong antiseptic solution, which was quite painful as it burned the skin. Clothing was also disinfected. People rarely got back their own clothes. In any case, the strong chemicals they used ruined the clothing so that what you got back was rags even if it had not been rags to start with. Such a disinfecting procedure lasted a minimum of eight hours but sometimes people had to stay overnight because there were simply too many people to handle.

One time, our family was taken in for disinfection. I managed to slip away from the marching column. When I returned home, my family was in bad shape. They were all lying around crying. Their heads had been shaven. My brother Pesach said he could not tolerate such an experience again. I tried to reassure them that their hair would grow back but they said it was not the hair, it was the degradation, the mistreatment.

At the beginning, people would buy their way out of these disinfection actions but as they became more frequent, the poorer people just gave in because they did not have enough money to buy themselves out again and again. My mother hid several times so that she, my sister, and I were disinfected only once while the other members of my family were disinfected twice.

8

It was now 1941. Conditions in the ghetto were awful. Crammed into its small area were thousands of people, starving, dying from typhus. Committees were established to help the poorest and the most helpless, particularly the children, especially the orphans. A former teacher who lived in our building, Zofia Szyfryn, put on plays with the children. Once they put on a performance of "Puss in Boots" in one of the apartments of our building. I prepared the stage decorations. I will never forget how she organized those pale and swollen children into lines of proud, singing marchers. The words they sang are forever inscribed in my memory:

Bo my jesteśmy młodzi,	For we are the young
I w tym jest nasza moc,	And this is our might,
I nic nas nie obchodzi,	Nothing bothers us,
Śpiewajmy dzień i noc!	Let us sing day and night

71

Świat młodzieży, świat młodzieży,	The world of youth, the world of youth,
Do nas cały świat należy!	The whole world belongs to us.

In the meantime, we were doing anything and everything we could do to bring bread into our home and stay alive. A shop in the ghetto, under the supervision of the Germans, went into business making rings for the *Wehrmacht* and the SS. These rings were made of brass, silver, gold, or platinum—precious metals stolen from Jews. One of the most popular ones was a silver ring with the deathhead, the skull emblem worn by the SS. They especially liked the tarnished silver effect. My father was hired by a friend to assist in this work. As a young man, he had made gold and silver chains in a jewelry factory to support himself while he studied music. Now he was back in the "jewelry business." For about two or three weeks, the whole family worked long hours in the apartment soldering and polishing the rings. What we earned enabled us to buy a subsistence diet: rotten cabbage, carrots, potatoes, and the like. We could not afford fruit or meat. Occasionally, my uncle Avraham Mendel, who still had contacts with meat smugglers, managed to send us some leftovers.

One afternoon, there was a knock at the door of our apartment. We were always afraid when someone knocked on the door, never knowing who was on the other side. I opened the door, and there stood two men. One introduced himself as a Mr. Zaleski, sent by my friend Izak Rubin, the lithographer. Zaleski, a Jew, had a highly intelligent face, with very shrewd eyes and a mustache. The other man was his partner. They asked me to do a favor, for which they would pay. They added that it was a matter of life and death.

In those days—and this was true before the war as well—everyone living in a building had to be registered with the local precinct. When you moved into a new apartment, the building superintendent gave you a certificate of residency indicating that you lived at your address, which you then had to have stamped at the local precinct within twenty-four hours. During the war, many people tried to get out of the ghetto and hide on the Aryan side. They needed such certificates of residency proving that they had the right to live where they claimed they did. Zaleski worked with an organized group selling these certificates to people hiding in the Aryan sector. He needed someone to produce them, so he turned to me.

As always, I consulted with my parents. Our decision was driven by both hunger and our consciences. Counterfeiting these certificates would pay for some food and maybe help some Jews hiding outside the ghetto as well. Zaleski set the price for each certificate at fifteen zlotys, enough to buy a bread. I accepted. I had no choice. It would keep us alive for a few more days. There was not much risk. We were condemned to death anyhow.

I worked with Zaleski for a short time. Then, he disappeared. Shortly afterwards, there came again a frightening pounding at our door. I was not home at the time. My mother opened the door to find three men standing there. They scared her because they threatened me. They said if I didn't submit to working with them, again "saving lives" (they were smuggling people out of the ghetto), I would pay for it dearly. We were scared. We didn't know where they came from, if they were Jewish gangsters, or had a Gestapo connection. If they were Gestapo, it would have meant death on the spot. I stayed away from my home for a week, hiding at my aunt's house, one block away. They came looking for me twice, and then they vanished, and never came again.

As time went on, there was a constant demand for life-saving documents: *Kennkarten,* the ID cards which all non-Jews carried, employment certificates, and permits to leave and reenter the ghetto. These were all essential for any Jew trying to survive on the Aryan side. One day, my friend Naftali Złoto approached me and asked me to help him counterfeit such documents. (Before the war, his father had owned a store that sold kerosene, paint, and chemicals. Soon after the ghetto was established, I heard that Naftali was smuggling kerosene into the ghetto.)

It was essential to have a complete original document from which to copy all the necessary details onto the forgery. Naftali was able to provide me with a few original blanks and photographs. Most important were the official seal of the particular office and the authorized signature. I had to reproduce all these details by hand, without any photographic or mechanical equipment. I had to improvise. One technique I used was to ink in the image on a piece of tracing paper, roll a hard-boiled egg over it to pick up the image, and then carefully roll the egg, which acted as a transfer, over the paper. (I used this technique for Zaleski. I had no egg, so he brought me a dozen, and told me to keep them and enjoy them once the job was finished. This meant another few days' survival.) At other times, I first traced the image onto tracing or wax paper, achieving a positive image (the image as it actually appears). Then I would turn the paper over and ink the negative image (i.e., the image in reverse, what you would see if you held it up to a mirror). All this had to be done with extreme precision, using drafting tools, a pen point, and stamping ink, which stays wet for some time. I could get a maximum of three imprints from any one tissue. Beyond that, the ink would be dry. For any additional stampings, I had to re-ink it all over again by hand. I was provided with only a limited number of blanks and had to be careful not to smudge or ruin them in any way. I applied this technique to stamped or printed signatures. Documents that had been signed by hand, rather than with a stamp, I had to counterfeit by hand.

At the proper moment, the inked drawing in the negative form was ready for the final transfer onto the document. The moment of the transfer of the imprint to the paper was critical: failure or victory? Most of the time, the imprints were fine.

The first ID card I prepared was for Naftali Złoto himself. His new name was Antoni Andrzej Świątkowski.

There was a demand for permits to leave and reenter the ghetto. I copied these from the very same certificate that I had received from Pommerenke, which I was still holding.

To forge some of these documents, I needed professional technical help. The help came from our devoted neighbor, Noah Czapnik, a well-known engraver and lithographer. Czapnik lived on the left-hand side of our building on the second floor. He was a man in his fifties, although to me he looked like he was seventy, he was so worn out.

Lithography is divided into three phases. I, as the artist, did the first step: preparing the artwork, designing the image and putting it onto the lithograph stone. The next step involved the chemical preparation of the stone for printing. Finally, the image had to be put on the press in order to transfer it from the stone onto paper. Czapnik was responsible for the chemical process and the printing.

We had no printing press, so Czapnik improvised an unusual invention. He used our clothing wringer, a manual wringer made in the United States, which had two rubber rollers. Once we had prepared the stone chemically and applied the ink to the design, he would open the wringer, and, instead of clothing, would put the stone with the paper between the two rollers. Then he would close the rollers with enough pressure and produce the print.

We worked in the cellar of our building, by the dim light of a homemade carbide lamp. Czapnik would remove the print from the "press," and we would look it over to check if it was clean and sharp. Sometimes only parts of the print came out because of the unevenness of the rollers. But often, the job was a success. The impression on the paper was good. (Noah Czapnik died of typhus in his home, shortly before the deportations of the Warsaw ghetto Jews to Treblinka began.)

My work carried a fearful responsibility. As much as my efforts might save a life, they might also end a life. It was painstaking work, but I got great satisfaction from it. It was a holy mission. Every stroke of the pen was like shooting the enemy. Every mark I made was revenge. My art was my weapon against my mortal enemy.

That summer, 1941, I was back working at the airfield, where there was a holiday atmosphere among the Germans. Germany had attacked the Soviet Union, and the fliers were drinking and singing in anticipation of their future victories. I was among a group of Jews assigned to paint and clean the canteen. The chief of the canteen, *Obergefreiter* Maus, handed me, as the artist, a special assignment. Under the arch in the main hall, I was to calligraph the following text: *In der Bibel, ist geschrieben, Du sollst auch deine Feinde lieben.* (In the Bible it is written, you should also love your enemies.) I was also to paint some decorative motifs on the walls. The job took several days. I did the calligraphy in black and red, the colors of the swastika. Painting this proverb was particularly painful to me. A committee of Germans had chosen it and I could not imagine what they had in mind: Were they joking? Could they reconcile their Christian beliefs with the horror all around us?

While I worked, some visitors, men and women in uniform, stopped by. They watched my progress with amazement, and expressed their approval in the usual German way, saying, "*Fabelhaft*" (excellent). I don't know if they knew who I was since my armband was folded up in my jacket, which I was not wearing while I worked.

There were several instances where the Germans expressed their grudging admiration for my work. One time, a high-ranking officer in the medical corps noticed me making a quick drawing in the sand with a stick. He came over and asked, "*Wie alt sind Sie?*" (How old are you?) I told him. He replied, "*Schade das Sie ein Jude sind.*" (Too bad you're a Jew.) I answered, "*Ich kann das nicht ändern.*" (I cannot change that.) He said, "*Na, ja,*" implying, "Yes, that's understandable," and walked away.

After our assignment at the canteen was finished, Jews were forbidden to enter it again.

Pommerenke was transferred to the Eastern front. Before he left, he gave me his golden watch, the same watch his grandfather had given him, for repair and safekeeping. He seemed to believe that, in some way, my holding it would ensure his safe return. I took the watch, brought it to the ghetto, had it repaired and kept it at home.

Pommerenke also introduced me to Lieutenant Hermann Lindeke from Leipzig who was head of the *Fahrbereit-schaft*, the unit that ran all the motorized vehicles at the airfield. Lindeke needed charts to keep track of the vehicles that were available at any given time, and I prepared these for him. I worked in his office, dressed in a pair of military overalls he had given me, so that I looked like a German soldier. Soldiers entering his office always gave the Heil Hitler salute. Lindeke told me not to respond with a Heil Hitler. Using this salute was unthinkable for a Jew. It would have been a terrible offense on my part. I responded to these salutes by just bowing my head.

He had set up a drafting table for me right next to his desk. I had the feeling that for some reason he wanted me near him. One day, after several weeks of working for him, he locked the door and asked me where exactly in the ghetto I lived. After I told him, he asked me whether I knew where Elektoralna Street was. I told him that I was a native of Warsaw and knew the ghetto very well. He then asked me whether I could keep my mouth shut. When I assured him that I could, he unlocked a drawer and told me to look inside. There was a gun there. He then said that if I told anyone what he was going to ask of me, there would be one bullet for me and one for him. I again assured him that I would tell no one. He said he would be back after lunch.

After lunch he came back with a canteen full of soup and a piece of bread and told me to eat my fill. He then took out a sealed envelope without an address and told me to deliver it to 32 Elektoralna Street, third floor, the door on the right. I was to knock three times on the door. He also gave me a package of pipe tobacco to be delivered to the people there. Their name was Rose.

He let me leave work early that day. When I got home, I steamed open the envelope with shaking hands, in the presence of my parents. The letter was addressed "To My Loved Ones" informing them of the sickness of a person known to them and expressing the hope that this person would recover speedily. It was signed by the letter "H" (Lindeke's first name was Hermann). I resealed the letter and went to deliver it.

I knocked on the door and an elderly gentleman who spoke German opened it. I told him that I had a letter from a supervisor where I worked. He took the letter into another room and I could hear several people discussing it. After the discussion, three persons appeared: the old gentleman, a woman who seemed to be his wife, and a young woman in her early thirties. They asked me where I lived and what I did. I told them that I worked at the airfield under Lindeke's supervision. They asked me how he was and I said he was well.

The following morning I reported to Lindeke that I had delivered his letter. A few days later he approached me and asked whether I could arrange to have the young woman brought out of the ghetto with a group of Jewish women workers and dropped off at a safe place where he could meet her. I discussed it with Eisenberg and he arranged it. I contacted the family and asked her to report for work at the *Judenrat*. She marched out of the ghetto with our work detail. Before entering the airfield, she left the unit and entered a grocery store owned by a man named Próchniak, a friendly and helpful Pole. This is the last I heard of this matter.

My impression is that Lindeke knew this family from Germany and wanted to help them. There may have been some family relationship between Lindeke and the Rose family but this is only speculation. I was very much afraid of being involved in this whole matter. Lindeke was known among the Germans and the Jews as the *Jüdischer Bluthund* (Jewish bloodhound) because of his behavior toward Jews. His screaming and threatening were terrible. I was afraid this was some kind of trap. But it turned out it was not.

One day, while I still worked for Lindeke, there was a knock at the door of the room where I worked. There stood Pommerenke, back from the Eastern front. Smiling as always, polite as always. He asked, "*Wie gehts?*" (How are things?) I replied, *"Danke, gut."* (Thank you, good.) He even stuck out his hand to shake hands with me. He asked for his watch. I said I would bring it back the next day, which I did.

My work for Lindeke came to an end when he was transferred. Pommerenke didn't need me at this time either because he was now a courier, traveling on orders of the army. However, he spoke to someone in the *Fahrkolonne* named *Stabsfeldwebel* Iven who had replaced Lieutenant von Buseck, telling him that I was a good worker and even suggesting to him, jokingly, that I could paint a portrait of his girlfriend.

Iven assigned me to the canteen. Jews had been barred from the canteen ever since the time of the German invasion of the Soviet Union and my sign had gone up reminding them to love their enemies. But Iven's order countermanded that. Maus, in charge of the canteen, did not like my being there, but there was nothing he could do about it, because the order had come from his superior. He greeted me every morning with *"Verdammter Judas, wie gehts?"* (Damned Judas, how are things?) He joked to one of his buddies, "Even if you kick this Judas out the front door, he'll come back through the back door."

I was assigned to clean the floors, dust the tables and chairs, keep the place tidy. This was a good job because it enabled me to hang out near the canteen where they prepared food packages for soldiers who had to travel. Sometimes, they gave me some leftovers. Mostly, however, it was not easy to get at the food. The storeroom where it was kept was always locked and supervised by Maus and his buddies.

Iven ordered me to do a portrait of his mistress whom he brought in to pose. She was a German woman but I don't know whether she was from Germany or was a *Volksdeutsche.* She came about twice a week for these sessions. I told Iven that I preferred to work with pastels in sepia colors, because these would bring out her highlights best. He got me the supplies. She loved the portrait. He didn't. He said I had made her look too young and pretty. I was scared because Iven struck me as being very unstable. On the one hand, he was a very efficient soldier. Everything had to be done perfectly according to the German motto *Befehl ist befehl* (order is order). Yet, he could suddenly become wild and hit somebody—and then let him go. He liked to scare people by screaming. And I was completely in his power; he could do anything he wanted to me. Luckily, he told me that I could continue working for him and that, if I wanted to, I could do his portrait. He would not sit for it; he had no patience for that. Instead, he gave me a photograph and told me to work from it. He was completely bald and he told me, laughing, that I could paint in a few hairs. He had rather a Semitic face and I knew I had to be careful to tone that down. I made sure to paint every detail of his uniform, every single insignia, correctly, because this meant a lot to all Germans. Fortunately, this portrait was a success.

Suddenly, our work at the airfield again came to a complete stop. No explanation was given.

There was a catastrophic hunger in our home. I remember one chilly, gray day, sometime in the autumn of 1941. I had managed to bring home some bread, a dark brown mixture of flour and sawdust. We put it on our little balance scale and divided it absolutely equally, each one standing around and watching to make sure, God forbid, that no one should have more or less than anyone else. I saw my brother Shlomo, an unbelievable man of justice, take a bit of his bread and knead it into my mother's piece. He did it secretly, so that she would not notice, because she would never have accepted it. It was an act of mercy, of justice, of devotion, so that she could live another hour. He did this on several occasions.

Friends advised us to visit a place where artists and literary figures gathered to receive a meal and make contact with "the world." The place was on Leszno Street, near the prewar Literary Club. Finally, one day, I went there with my father and my brother, Pesach.

The meal was served by a group of volunteer ladies, representing the elegance and aristocracy of prewar Jewish Warsaw. I saw some of my father's friends and colleagues sitting at the tables: Mr. Stromberg, chief clarinet soloist of the Warsaw Opera, Mr. Lewinson, master violinist, and others whose faces were almost unrecognizable. People were sitting and sipping soup, holding a piece of bread in their shaking hands. We ate with bowed heads. Each one was ashamed in front of the other. There was total silence.

We never went back again.

9

The winter of 1941–1942 was a severe one. Typhus raged in the ghetto. Hundreds died from this devastating disease. There was nothing to fight it with, no medicine, no food, no sanitary conditions. Every building set up a committee to help the sick, remove the dead, do whatever it could with their meager means. The tenants of our building selected Gutmacher, a well-known socialist, as the chairman, because he was the most prominent person among us. A number of other people volunteered to help him, including Mrs. Szyfryn, the teacher, her husband, a dental technician, and my father. A well-known and respected *felczer*, a paramedic, by the name of Zając, assisted us whenever he could. There were still some doctors in the ghetto, but they could not do much with their severely limited resources. In addition, they, and all the intellectuals, lived in fear and hiding, because they were special targets of the Gestapo seeking to destroy any potential leadership among the Jewish population. One Sunday in January, 1942, the Gestapo carried out a raid on all these prominent people in the ghetto, going from house to house according to a list. Dr. Zygmunt Sztajnkalk, our beloved family doctor, who had treated us since we were born, was shot in front of his building at 17 Nowolipki Street. Others survived this raid but were later deported. One of these was Dr. S. Pupko, one of the great humanitarians of prewar Jewish Warsaw. An orthodox Jew and medical doctor, he always helped the Jewish underprivileged. He was deported to the concentration camp Budzyń.

All of us became ill that winter, one after the other. My father got sick first, followed by Pesach, then Esther, then my mother, then Shlomo. Everyone did their best to help the others, until they too became ill. The sickness starts with red dots on the skin, headache, and a very high fever, reaching 40, 41 degrees Celsius (104–105 degrees Fahrenheit). The first few days you are mostly unconscious. Your tongue dries up, and you need to be given water. We had no water; it froze in the pipes. There was no heat, because there was no coal and no gas. We embraced frozen pots of water to our burning bodies, to cool the fever, and to melt the ice. The nights in particular were nightmares. I was the strongest, the last to get sick. Until then, I was trying to help them, but how much could I do? I kept putting ice—the one thing we had plenty of—on their heads to cool them. One morning I saw that Pesach was unconscious, dying. I kept massaging him, trying to restore him to life. The *felczer* Zając gave him an injection of glucose that he had smuggled in somehow. Mrs. Szyfryn (who ultimately survived Auschwitz) helped us, and my aunts, Bela and Pesa, brought us a warm meal, some soup, whenever they could. Pesa's husband, my uncle Avraham Mendel, who also got typhus, said that he was only sorry that the disease didn't kill us all and spare us from further, as yet unknown, horrors. We kept our door locked because the Germans considered the sick a menace to the community, and the Jewish police were always on the lookout for sick people, to quarantine them. Once you were taken away to these "disinfection stations," you never returned. A number of times we heard knocking on the door, but we didn't answer.

I was the first to recuperate, to go out and look for food. I hardly made it to my friend Naftali Złoto's house, taking along my father's old Kodak camera and my briefcase, which was still in good condition. He did not want to take these things from me but I insisted. He gave me some bread, which was all he had at home. I soaked it in water with some salt and made some kind of soup that I fed to my family.

We were sick for weeks, until the middle of January. We all survived the illness. We were now immune to it forever.

As the days and weeks passed, winter turning into spring, into summer, we struggled to stay alive. We had nothing left at home to barter or sell. The few things we still owned, like our old candelabrum, were either too bulky to smuggle out of the ghetto or completely worthless. My mother's wedding ring was long gone, sold. The little silver ring which my father had given her as an engagement ring had been stolen off her finger while she lay unconscious with typhus. People had been going in and out of our apartment, and I had also been sick at that time, so I had not known what was going on. Our musical instruments had already been confiscated by the Germans, who promised that we would get them back after the war. (Just like my father's colleague, Zofia Wierchowska, who promised to pay us back money she owed "after the war.") My brother, Pesach, could barely do anything. In the beginning, he had earned a few zlotys by substituting for other poor souls who could not work, but he was too weak to do that any more. My younger brother, Shlomo, was too sick, too weak, as well. They looked like skeletons, with swollen legs. I would press the swollen skin with my fingertips and see how long it took for the indentation to subside, to judge the extent of starvation. I had become an "expert diagnostician."

We relied on help from my aunt Pesa and on whatever I could scavenge from the Aryan sector or the airfield, where there was only sporadic work. I did some odd jobs here and there in ghetto. Some I got from my loyal friend, Izak Rubin who worked for the last lithography shop left in the ghetto (the rest had all been liquidated). I earned a few zlotys, enough to get by for another day or two. In addition, we still had some ration tickets, but, because we had no money, every time I got some food (a bread or some marmalade), I had to give away half of it to pay for it.

Under these severe circumstances, during these darkest days in the ghetto, my mother blessed me. I want to record this particular blessing which she gave me before she was taken away into eternity. "May you find favor in the eyes of God and man," she said, and then she added, "and in the eyes of the enemy." She also prayed that if I survived, it should be God's will that I find her brother Mendel in America, or my cousin Mordechai Leib in Uruguay.

It was now July, 1942. The turmoil in the ghetto was very great. Announcements were made all over the ghetto that the Jews were being "resettled" to labor camps in the East in order to improve conditions for everyone. Posters were pasted all over telling us to get ready for the trip. Those who voluntarily appeared for resettlement at the *Umschlagplatz*, the assembly point from which the transports left, would be allowed to take along for the journey up to fifteen kilograms of personal belongings, plus money and jewelry. They would also be given extra rations of bread and marmalade. A Jew who worked for any German establishment would receive a certificate exempting his or her family from resettlement.

Nobody knew what to believe. We lived, every minute, under the threat of death. We lived on rumors, from moment to moment. There was nothing to lean on. We didn't know what was a lie, what was the truth. We knew only what we saw. All the rest, our entire existence, was a big question mark.

In the midst of all this confusion, we heard rumors that there might be a resumption of work at the airfield at Okęcie. I went to Eisenberg, the head of the Jewish workers at Okęcie and, with tears in my eyes, begged him to take me back to work there. Eisenberg said he would do his best. He told me to report the following morning to the workers' assembly point at Leszno Street, across from the Supreme Court of Warsaw, near the main gate of the ghetto. From there, trolley cars would take the workers away to work, and he believed that I would be going along.

The following day was July 22, *Erev Tisha B'Av* (the eve of the ninth day of the Jewish month of Av), Wednesday, a rainy morning. All of Nature cried with the Jewish population over the destruction of our Temple in Jerusalem two thousand years ago. And we were facing destruction again.

My mother could not believe that I might get work at the airfield. This would be a miracle: not only would it get me out of the ghetto, but it would be the means of protecting my entire family, because I would get one of these precious certificates promising not to resettle the family of anyone working for the Germans. To be sure that I would indeed be accepted into the work force going to the airfield, she accompanied me to the assembly point.

They loaded us onto trolley cars on Leszno Street and I could see my mother waving at me as the trolley left. Her face was pale and tears were rolling down her swollen cheeks. She even put on her black-framed pair of glasses to see me better—the details I remember because this is one of the most tragic moments in my life. I looked at her, the trolley moved, and she disappeared from my sight. This was the last time I saw her.

Returning to the ghetto that evening, my work group of about eighty Jews got as far as the Gęsia Street gate, across the street from the Jewish cemetery. We were searched, beaten, and ordered to lie face down and wait for further orders. We saw people being driven into the cemetery. Some rode on horse-drawn wagons, others were on foot. We could hear screams and moans and then we heard machine-gun fire. After things quieted down, they ordered our group into the cemetery. They gave us shovels and under terrible blows we were ordered to cover the 400 to 450 bodies with lime and then a thin layer of earth. When we were finished we were driven back into the ghetto.

Why did the Germans have to massacre these people at the Warsaw cemetery when they were going to kill them anyhow? They did it to fool us, to subdue us even further, to prove that everything they said was true. They made it look as though only those who were useless, who couldn't work, or who were guilty of disobedience or causing trouble would be killed at the cemetery. The trains and transports really were for resettlement, just as they promised. They even made the Jews set up a little infirmary at the *Umschlagplatz*, staffed by nurses, to care for those who felt weak when they got to the *Umschlagplatz*, give them a little drink of water, reassure them. They did all this to maintain these miserable illusions, to play this sadistic game with us. And we believed it. We wanted to believe anything. We wanted to believe their lies even though we knew they were lies. We heard that people being taken to work never returned, and that there was killing going on. We heard that the Jewish community of Lublin was devastated in 1941, that there was no trace of the Jews there. But we did not expect this to happen to Warsaw. And we were only beginning to hear rumors about what was going on in Treblinka.

Just inside the ghetto gate I met my friend David Gingold, a fellow student from the art school, two grades ahead of me. He had been waiting for my return in order to pass on a message from my family: my mother had never returned from escorting me to Leszno Street that morning, and was probably being held at the *Umschlagplatz*.

This particular day I had been working—unloading cases of champagne—at the airfield and had fallen off a truck, injuring my right ankle, which had become swollen. I limped home and was met by my father, my sister, and my brothers. Our mother was gone. It was the first time I ever saw my father cry.

Later that evening, I went down to the Wajnberg family whose son was a Jewish policeman in the ghetto. In the beginning, it was the Jewish police, under SS and Ukrainian supervision, who dragged the Jews out of their homes to be deported. Each Jewish policeman had a quota of six lives to be delivered daily to the *Umschlagplatz*. If they did not fill their quota, they and their families could be taken away.

They would march through the streets in companies, like a wedge, like you clear snow. Then they would disperse into the houses, running up the stairs and into the apartments, screaming, and brutally forcing the people out. Many of them were merciless, pulling women out by their hair, throwing people down the stairs. Crouching on our little balcony, I saw one policeman rip a child away from his mother and throw him onto a wagon, making the mother, half crazed, run after it, trying to be reunited with her child.

(It was almost impossible to find one another again, if people became separated. Thousands of people were being pushed toward the trains. It was a madhouse.) Invalids were dragged through the streets by the crooks of their own canes. The streets were filled with piles of discarded canes.

Wajnberg's son admitted that he had seen my mother being rounded up, and had advised her to hide in the courtyard of one of the buildings with a group of Jews. He claimed that he went back to rescue her, but by then she was gone. I didn't—and don't—believe him. I hold him responsible for her capture. I believe he could have saved my mother that day, had he really wanted to.

We spent a sleepless night crying. My sister applied compresses to my foot all night long because I had to go back to work the next day.

My plan, the next morning, was to enter the *Umschlagplatz* to look for my mother. But the *Luftwaffe* guard escorting my work group, *Obergefreiter* Fischer (a different Fischer from the others I have previously mentioned) refused to let me go. He promised to help me in the evening on our way back from the airfield. He kept his promise. In the evening, after discharging my group of workers into the ghetto, he received permission from the SS guard at the ghetto gate to escort me to the *Umschlagplatz,* just around the corner.

At the *Umschlagplatz,* three SS officers with whips were standing. Fischer told them that the Jew he was escorting thought that his mother was inside the building. One of the SS men laughed and said: "*Sie alle kommen dahin.*" (You all will get there.) But he let me enter the building. Fischer waited outside for me.

It was horrible. The place was full of urine and feces, with dead bodies and sick people all over. On the second floor, I recognized a musician by the name of Katz. He sat, half-dead, against the wall. He said he had been there two days and had seen my mother earlier that day but she had been driven to the ramps leading to the trains.

I left the building with the help of Fischer who pulled me out against the will of some Jewish policemen who didn't want to let me leave the building. *"Ich bin Deutscher, und ich bestimme"* (I am German, and I decide), he told them. Outside, the three SS officers were still standing there, still laughing at me. Fischer escorted me home. I offered him a reward, my brother Pesach's watch, which had been his bar-mitzvah gift from our uncle Boruch. Pesach had given it to me to exchange for food but so far the opportunity to do so had never presented itself. Fischer refused to accept the watch. I returned home and told my family what had happened.

Four days after my mother's deportation, I returned home from the airfield to find the apartment empty. Because of the curfew, I could not do anything until the next morning. On the way to the airfield, Fischer made my work group wait at the exit from the ghetto while he again accompanied me to the *Umschlagplatz*. Through a window, I saw my father, my sister, and my brothers in the building, making frantic motions to me. I tried to enter the building but the Jewish policeman stationed there said he would not let them out and, in fact, if I persisted, he would pull me into the building as well. My German escort, Fischer, intervened and ordered him to let my family out. He obeyed, and my family went back home. It turned out that they had reported to the *Umschlagplatz* voluntarily because they were so hungry that they could not bear it any more. They had been given the bread and marmalade promised to those reporting voluntarily for resettlement, and even managed to take this home with them.

Several days later, I received a document at the airfield that was supposed to protect my family from deportation. We pasted it, as ordered, on the door of our apartment. It stated: "The family of the above-named Jew, employed by the German military, is absolved from being resettled." It was signed by the District *Kommandant* of the SS, Department of Labor, Jewish District, Warsaw.

It was a lie. It did not protect anybody.

The Germans now decided that Jews working at the airfield, about 130 to 140 of us, would no longer be returned to the ghetto at the end of each workday. They explained that this decision had to do with the unsettled conditions in the ghetto where the Germans were busy deporting anyone who was useless, or disabled, or otherwise could not fulfill their obligation by working for the Germans. If they returned us to the ghetto each night, we might accidentally be resettled with the others. They wanted to keep us—their chosen ones, who were familiar with the work—together, so the work would not suffer. Therefore, as of August 5, 1942, we were to report to work with clothing and whatever we could carry because from now on we would sleep at the airfield.

Now came one of the most difficult moments in my life. All these terrible days, all these months, I had guarded my family. Now I had to make a decision: should I obey the order to report for work—after all, they knew my name, they had it on the list—and be kept at the airfield, or stay in the ghetto with my family? For many hours, my father, my sister, my brothers, and I sat and discussed our options, what would happen if I left, if I stayed. I could not take them with me: my brothers and sister were too weak (and they were no longer taking women workers at this time) and my father was too old. They said, "Listen. If you stay with us, we may all have to report to the *Umschlagplatz*, because there is no way to survive without bread, without anything. On the other hand, if you go to work, there's a chance that you may still help us, by bringing us some food, by having that certificate of protection." I decided to return to the airfield. On the morning of August 5, 1942, I said good-bye to them. It was an emotional good-bye—we kissed each other, we hugged each other—and I left. They remained in the apartment. I thought I would see them again in a day or two. Deep in my heart, I wanted to believe that the plan to keep us at the airport was just temporary. I did not realize that this would be the last time I saw my family. I still did not realize what kind of horrible situation we were in. I was naïve. My mind did not comprehend the immensity of the tragedy. We all thought that eventually these deportations would stop. How many people could the Germans take away, after all?

But, at the end of work that day, when they marched us over to the barracks where we were to be kept, about a kilometer outside the airfield, I was scared to death. Because these were military barracks, with one big gate, with watchtowers and barbed wire, built specifically to house prisoners. (In fact, Russian POWs were imprisoned in barracks across from us; we were forbidden to communicate with them.) A big sign warned that leaving the barracks without permission was punishable by death. I did not have my exit pass any more; it had been confiscated.

We were desperate, trapped with no more links with the ghetto, with our families. We had no idea what was happening to them. We kept working at the airfield during the day, sleeping in the barracks at night, with no news, no sources of information. I was scared to death to ask any German what was going on. The only information we got about the drama inside the ghetto came from a few people who had been hiding in the Aryan sector, or who had been working for some factories in the ghetto or outside, and who managed to join our groups at the airfield. They gave us the general picture:

that thousands of Jews were being taken away. But even they did not know specifics about what happened to whom. I did not expect to see my family again. I just could not imagine how they could survive.

10

Suddenly, around Yom Kippur, the storm stopped. A stillness fell on the ghetto. The Germans halted the mass deportations, claiming that the ghetto had been reduced for reasons of productivity. The remaining population would be registered and employed in German-run shops established to produce goods for the Reich, like tailor shops making clothing and uniforms, shoe factories, and a number of other industries.

To the Germans, the ghetto was a place of treasure. Almost all the Jews were gone. Their apartments were deserted. The few Jews who were left were formed into special units, *Werterfassung,* responsible for entering the deserted buildings and confiscating and gathering all valuable goods. After all, the people were gone, the possessions belonged to the Third Reich. These units prepared tons of objects—

clothing, artwork, shoes, silverware, furniture, beds, blankets—for shipment to Germany.

Many Germans wanted to take part in these operations. However, Jews, and Jewish belongings, were the property of the highest echelon of the German government, the Gestapo and the SS. The *Wehrmacht* and the *Luftwaffe* had no right to enter the ghetto and handle Jewish property without permission from the SS. Getting such permission was easy. All they had to do was state that they had to bring their Jewish laborers into the ghetto to find suitable clothing for the upcoming winter months. Once there, it was a simple matter to order the Jews to steal for them whatever they could find in the empty apartments. They were particularly interested in leather, jewelry, and textiles.

Like many soldiers, Pommerenke was anxious to enter the ghetto and see what was happening there. He loaded about fifteen or twenty of us onto a big wagon with some German escorts and we entered the ghetto. We got to my building, since Pommerenke expressed an interest in seeing how I lived. One of the Germans, the driver, stayed below with the wagon. The rest of us entered the building.

All the doors to all the apartments were open, swinging by creaking hinges in the wintry drafts. Curtains floated through the windows. On the steps, you could see spots of blood from the bodies of people who had been shot and dragged down the stairs. There were valises all over the backyard, and broken chairs. A spoon lay on the floor. It was like wild animals had torn everything apart.

Pommerenke, with two or three soldiers, was walking from apartment to apartment, sniffing out what remained to be taken. I jumped on ahead, running like lightning up to the third floor, to our apartment, Number 18, which was straight ahead on the landing. The door to our apartment was open. I ran inside.

The windows in the apartment were open. My mother's curtains were still there, torn, dirty, billowing in the wind. The apartment was full of feathers. When the Germans ransacked an apartment, they would slice through the feather comforters on the beds. Feathers were floating like snow, and the draft carried them all over.

Straight ahead, through a little hallway, was the kitchen. My banjo, which I had designed myself, was still there, under the window, near the cabinet. The skin was ripped apart and the strings were gone, but the round wooden body and the metal frame were still intact. I went into a terrifying fury and smashed it into pieces. I smashed it out of rebellion, desperation, anger, madness, as though I could kill the enemy, punish the enemy, by doing so. Like Samson: "*Tamut nafshi im plishtim.*" (Let my soul die with the Philistines.) Life is gone, everything is gone, this had no right to exist any further. Something that had been dear to me would not be dear to anybody else. Not you, not me, *nobody's* going to enjoy it. It was a moment of instinctive terrifying violence, the only violent outlet I had in that lightning moment when I moved through the apartment. I smashed the banjo, and left it there, smashed.

I went into the living room, with its floor-to-ceiling tiled oven in the left-hand corner. I opened the little door to the oven, and in the ashes I found the treasure I had hidden there a few months earlier: the little thread-cutter we had used to make screws for musical instruments. I put it in my pocket. This represented a few zlotys value. (I sold it later to a locksmith in the Aryan sector. He looked at me with pity and gave me fifteen zlotys, which was good enough for me.)

I ran into the bedroom, to the left of the living room. When I reached the closet in the bedroom, my first impulse was to look for a small box, a highly polished little mahogany chest, where we kept photographs and other little family treasures. The box was there, its lid missing. I went through this like lightning and found several loose photographs, of my mother, my father, and the one of me with my brothers and sister. I gathered them up and shoved them in my breast pocket. I looked for my father's diary. It was gone. The only other thing I found was a pair of *tfillin* (phylacteries). I didn't remember to whom they belonged, because I was in a daze and confused. I just dumped them into my pockets.

On the floor, near the bed, I saw a stream of black blood, that started from the sack of straw we had slept on and reached almost to the door of the bedroom. It scared me; I didn't know what had happened. But there was nobody to ask, nobody to answer. I just saw it, registered it in my memory. There was no time to think about anything because fast steps were approaching.

My smashing and knocking had apparently aroused the interest of the Germans below. They started yelling, "*Was ist los?*" (What is happening?) By this time, Pommerenke reached our apartment, with his whip in his hand. He wanted to see how I lived. He looked around, and noticed that above the closet—I hadn't even noticed it—there was something wrapped in newspapers and tied with string. He pointed at it and asked, "*Was ist dort?*" (What is over there?) I told him, "Dishes." These were our special porcelain Passover dishes. He ordered, "*Herunternehmen!*" (Take it down!) I climbed up on a chair, took it down, and he said, "*Vorsicht!*" (Careful!) The package was carried downstairs and loaded onto the wagon.

He had also ordered us to take clothing. Whatever

schmattes I could find, I took along. I had no interest in any material goods. They meant nothing to me. I just looked to get the hell out of there, because I was completely destroyed. My blood pressure must have been near bursting. Can you imagine, you come into your apartment, where you had a life, and all you see is a stream of blood?

And what of this German, this "nice guy" who had treated me decently at the airfield? At the time, there was no time to think about anything. But now, I look at the circumstances, and want to analyze them, to understand: was he decent? Was he normal? Did he understand my position, that my family was gone, that everything was destroyed? Did he realize that he was committing a violent, physical attack on a home, *my* home, before my very eyes? Because that's exactly what he did, without thinking twice, completely matter-of-fact. It belonged to him. Everything in the ghetto belonged to him, to them. Obviously, I could not take these material goods with me. But did he even think to suggest: "pack it up, and sell it, and keep the money for yourself, you may need it?"

There was a total disregard for my feelings, because I was not supposed to have any feelings. I was only an object. I would serve him, I would please him by doing art. Otherwise, I was nobody for him. And the only way I could react was by not thinking. There was no thinking. You had no time to evaluate anything, because you were constantly in motion, in a constant fight for your life, like an animal. You moved around in terrible fear, you didn't know what might happen next. Today, looking back, I have time to try to analyze things and create a theory. But back then, when it happened, you had no time to think. You are being attacked by someone who wants to kill you. You think only how to get out of the situation. You don't think about food, you don't think about water, you don't think about where you are going to sleep. You react by instinct, do whatever you need to do to get through the situation. Whatever you see, whatever you experience, you just take it into your mind and into your heart, and you keep moving, to survive a little longer, and that's all.

For several hours, we continued down the street to other deserted Jewish homes, loaded more things onto the wagon, and then went back to Okęcie.

A week or so later, some other *Luftwaffe* officers again decided to return to the ghetto, so that we could get "more clothing." I went along again.

Most of the ghetto, which the Jews now called the "wild ghetto," was deserted. Your footsteps echoed through the streets. Your life was in danger. If you were caught walking there without a military escort, or a special *Ausweiss* (I.D. card), you could be shot on sight. The German soldiers who brought us into the ghetto and left us there didn't care that we were in danger. They gave us orders to get them leather goods, and textiles, and that was that. We had to find our own way.

I moved carefully through the streets, hugging the wall. Sometimes I went up on the roofs of the buildings and went from building to building, rooftop to rooftop, inching my way toward the area where the remaining Jews were concentrated, working for German shops. Nearby were the brush-making shops, on Świętojerska Street. I entered Nowolipie Street. Suddenly, I saw a familiar face: Yankel, my mother's younger brother. When he saw me, we embraced and started crying. He said to me, "You have a brother!" My brother Pesach was alive.

Yankel told me that he had lost his wife, Frimet, and their two children, Chana and Moshe, in the deportations. All three of his brothers, my uncles, had also been taken: Hershel with his wife Miriam and their two children, Velvel and his wife Justina and their two children, Isser and his wife and three children. My uncle Boruch was still in Argentina, safe. But his wife, Eva, and their children, Chana and David, had also been taken to Treblinka.

Life in the ghetto after the deportations was wild, beyond any law, any order. People lived like animals. They were in a daze. You met a brother in the street, you kissed him, and you hugged him, and you lost him. You didn't even think about him. You were just one unit, one entity, yourself, anxious to survive. Everybody was running to save his own life. To survive for what, you didn't know, but just not to be strangled, not to be shot, not to be killed, not to finish your life. I am not in a position to explain it, just to describe it. To me it was a horror, a wild orgy of life before death. So when I saw my uncle, the reunion was very emotional, but then we fell away from each other, like blocks of ice. I left him and went to find my brother. I never saw my uncle again after that.

My uncle had pointed to a building on the even-numbered side of Nowolipie Street. I entered the building, ran up to the second floor, to an apartment on the right, and knocked at the door. I heard a voice. I started screaming, "Pesach, open!" He opened the door. It was a greeting of horror, joy, pain, all together; I don't know how you mix all these ingredients together.

He told me what had happened to our family after I had left the ghetto to stay at the airfield in August. They were holding onto each other, hunting from one deserted apartment to another, living off whatever scraps they could find, like starving cats roaming around garbage cans, surviving from minute to minute. Then, before Yom Kippur, 1942, the order came from the German High Command to finish the job, to clear the ghetto of all the Jews. It was a massive deportation, carried out by the SS, with all their helpers: Lithuanians, Ukrainians, Latvians, and other bandits. By that time, the Jewish police did not play much of a role. They were no longer trusted.

People were taken en masse—my father, brothers and sister among them—and driven through the streets in this avalanche toward the *Umschlagplatz*. They were pushing them through Wołyńska Street, a poor little street where my uncle Isser had a little butcher shop. Somewhere there, in the midst of all the confusion, Pesach lost sight of the rest of the family. He started running for his life, because while they were herding the people through, they were also shooting, and dozens of people were killed on the spot. He ran down into a basement and found dead bodies there. He lay down among the bodies, amid the terrible smell, until the noises from the street died down. He stayed there close to a week, scavenging in the basement and in some of the deserted apartments. He lived off some grains, animal feed he found there. There was no electricity, no gas, and no water; it had all been shut off. The only liquid he had was a little alcohol left in some bottles he came across in an apartment. He started drinking because he was desperately thirsty, and his body started swelling up. When I found him, his body was swollen and he had difficulty urinating. He cried continuously, an endless lamentation: "What's going to happen to us?"

I asked him, "how do you live?" He explained that eventually he had made his way to the area around Nowolipie Street, where the last remaining Jews still lived. Most of them worked in German-run shops under the control of big civilian organizations like Toebbens and Schultz and others, and were therefore still entitled to get ration tickets. Pesach, as a "wild" inhabitant of the ghetto, had no way to get food. He managed to counterfeit a few ration tickets in order to get some bread. He told me he had learned how to do it from watching me.

He also explained the stream of black blood I had found on the floor of the bedroom in our apartment. Shortly after the rest of the family had been taken away, Pesach had come back to see what was left of our apartment. The doors were wide open. On the floor in the bedroom, lying in pools of blood, were our cousin, Josef Dov Flamm and his wife, Golde. They had apparently taken refuge in our apartment and were murdered there, shot by Germans or Ukrainians. Pesach dragged the bodies down the stairs, loaded them onto a flat two-wheeled cart and pulled them to the cemetery for burial. He was helped by another illegal inhabitant of the ghetto living in our building, a street-boy whom we called *dos hentl* (the hand—he was a pickpocket). The Germans didn't usually interfere with burial squads taking corpses to the cemetery outside the ghetto.

Pesach found a Waltham pocket watch on Flamm's body with his name engraved on it in Hebrew letters. He gave it to me. I told him to be patient, that I was going back to the airfield, and would do whatever I could to help him.

I immediately decided that I must get Pesach to join me at the airfield. At that time, I was working on a big portrait of the commander of the barracks, Lieutenant Schultze. Working from a photograph, I was drawing a portrait of him using a special black-and-white lithograph technique I had mastered. I told Schultze that my brother was living in the ghetto and asked if it would be possible to have him join me at the airfield. Several days later, Licht, the *Lageraelteste* (the Jewish head of the Jewish prisoners at the airfield, responsible for carrying out all German orders) entered the ghetto again with some Germans who wanted to rob more things. On that occasion, Licht, under orders from Schultze, met my brother and brought him back to the airfield with him. Pesach was permitted to work with me at my tasks, which consisted of all kinds of manual labor such as unloading railroad cars, digging ditches, and construction. He was weak and could not do much.

When winter closed in on us, Pesach could not work in the cold. I arranged with Licht for him to stay in the barracks where he did some cleaning. He was coughing up blood. Early in 1943, I managed to get Pesach away from the airfield to the grocery store of Próchniak where a Polish doctor by the name of Kozłowski examined him and diagnosed tuberculosis in both lungs. He gave him some medicine but, of course, it was of no use. I will always be grateful to both Próchniak and Kozłowski for their humanity in risking their own lives to examine my brother.

11

In January, 1943, the Germans at the airport decided to take a few of us—including Pesach and me—back into the ghetto to get warm clothing to survive the frigid winter. They would take us in by wagon and leave us to gather whatever we could find before being picked up again two days later. And as long as we were already there, and because we supposedly knew all the hiding places in the ghetto, we were supposed to steal leather goods and textiles for the soldiers who escorted us.

We entered the ghetto on January 15 in the late afternoon and were dismissed. Everyone went off in a different direction. Pesach and I spent the time looking for people we knew. We found our aunt Pesa and her son Moshe on Święto-jerska Street, where the brushmaking shops were located. She told me that her husband Avraham Mendel, the meat supplier, had been caught during the massive deportation, with only forty zlotys in his pocket. She never heard from him again. She informed us that our youngest aunt, Bela, who had gotten married after the Warsaw ghetto was established, now lived on Miła Street. We found her as well. Everyone expressed the hope that we would somehow survive. After a day, or a day and a half there, we decided to see what was happening in other sections of the ghetto, and went to Niska Street, where the units of Jews gathering and sorting the confiscated goods (*Werterfassung*) lived. David Gingold, my friend from the Piłsudski school, lived at 12 Niska Street with his family. We stayed overnight in his home.

It was now January 18. We had been ordered to gather at the gate near the *Umschlagplatz* at six o'clock in the morning, and a Luftwaffe escort was supposed to meet us about seven o'clock to take us back to the airport. Pesach and I walked along Zamenhofa Street toward the point of assembly. Suddenly, like a storm, people were running toward us on Zamenhofa, away from the ghetto gate. There was panic. People yelled at us: "Retreat! They are rounding up Jews!" I heard shooting. I found out later that the Germans had intended this to be the final liquidation of the ghetto. But for the first time, the Warsaw Ghetto fighters retaliated, to let the Germans know that they couldn't get away with their actions with impunity any longer. However, this first attempt at an uprising failed. There was a massacre and the Germans rounded up six thousand Jews and sent them off to their deaths in Treblinka.

My brother and I retreated to Gingold's apartment on Niska Street. We didn't know what to do. Meanwhile, the whole street was surrounded by SS, standing with machine gun nests. They ordered everyone to go down to the street, warning that anyone found in the apartments would be shot on sight. They lined people up for a selection to see who really belonged there and who did not. Up in Gingold's apartment, I quickly managed to counterfeit red little badges indicating that we lived there. We went down to the street and went through the selection. We managed to survive it.

Of the twenty men who had come into the ghetto, now only eight of us were left, including my brother and a friend, Jurek (George) Topas. It was now about two or three o'clock in the afternoon. I decided I had to do something to survive. I would go to the local Number 4 Precinct at 10 Niska Street, and try to call Lieutenant Schultze, the head of the prison camp at Okęcie, for whom I was drawing a portrait. The people I was with laughed at me. They thought I was a fool. I went anyway.

There were masses of people at the gate of the precinct trying to get in to make calls to any contacts they had on the Aryan side, to sound the alarm that they were trapped. I pushed my way to the gate. The policeman standing there asked me what I wanted. I said, "I must call the headquarters of the airfield in Warsaw." He seemed surprised, and asked me if I was serious. I said "yes" and he let me in. The sergeant sitting inside asked what my business was with the airfield. I said that I had to talk with the commander of our unit. He told me to go ahead and make the call. I picked up the phone. A female voice from the Warsaw telephone company answered. I spoke to her in German and in Polish and she thought I was a German. She hooked me up immediately with the office of the barracks at the airfield. I asked—in German—to speak with Lieutenant Schultze. A male voice answered and said he was not there, but he listened to me and said he would call Licht, the Jewish head of the Jewish prisoners at Okęcie, who had remained in the barracks. I waited several minutes, and finally Licht picked up the phone.

"What's happening?"

I told him, in Yiddish, "*Es iz a brokh.* (It's a tragedy.) We are trapped."

He took down our exact location: 12 Niska Street, third floor, with the Gingold family. He spoke to some soldiers and then said to me, "We will come to pick you up, not today any more, because it's too late, but tomorrow morning."

I came back to Gingold's apartment where the whole group was waiting anxiously for me. When I told them Licht had said he would come for us, they laughed at me and told me I was nuts. This will never happen, they said. It's a fantasy, an illusion. You are trapped. I said, "Let's wait and see." We waited in fear all night. All night, I wondered, did I make a fool of myself? Or will this really happen?

About 6:30 the next morning, I heard someone yelling from the courtyard. "Wyszogrod! Wyszogrod!" I looked down into the yard and saw Licht standing with a group of soldiers. They had come to pick us up.

They marched us along Zamenhofa toward the gate of the ghetto near the *Umschlagplatz.* At the gate, the German guards took us inside the guardhouse and searched us one by one from head to toe. From the windows of the building, we heard the desperate screams of a number of Jews—including some from our work group who'd been caught in the selection—who recognized us and were begging, "Save us! Licht, save us, we are here!" Licht tried to intervene but the SS guards said, "No. If you enter, you'll never come out." With bowed heads, we left under the escort of the soldiers, walking along Okopowa Street, which is the continuation of the street where the Jewish cemetery is. We came to a bar where they called a halt. They took us inside, put us in a corner, had a few drinks—not offering us anything, of course—and then brought us back to Okęcie.

When we got back to the airfield, there was bewilderment and amazement that we were still alive. This was the miracle of January 18, 1943. For those brief moments, *my* power prevailed, my way of talking, my managing to impress the Polish sergeant enough to let me go in, pick up the phone, and make that call. In that instant, I saved my life, I saved my brother's life, and a few other lives. These were the situations where some miracle spared you from death, and you were able to go on again, until the next miracle, and the next.

(George Topas is the only surviving witness of this incident besides me. He lives in the United States with his family.)

In March, 1943, Pesach's condition deteriorated and he began having seizures. Even under these circumstances, his psychological condition remained good. Pesach was a very intelligent person with a great sense of humor. One day, he was assigned to clean the latrines behind the barracks, a very unpleasant job. He put the word out that money could be made by selling the feces to the peasants as fertilizer. Several Jews volunteered to help him and were furious when they discovered that he had fooled them.

I was again working for *Stabsfeldwebel* Iven at the *Fahrkolonne,* cleaning floors, chopping wood, shining boots, and washing the soldiers' dirt. Pesach worked for him, too. One day, in the spring of 1943, my brother had another seizure. Iven noticed it and ordered that he be transferred to the ghetto hospital. I could not keep him with me at the airfield anymore. Licht, accompanied by an armed German guard, took Pesach to the Jewish Hospital at 6 Gęsia Street. I tried to go along but the guard ordered me to step back. My brother tried to comfort me. "Don't worry," he said. "It'll be fine." Helpless, I watched as my brother was taken away.

A week later I spoke with Schultze, the lieutenant in

charge of the barracks, and he agreed to escort me into the ghetto to visit my brother. He hinted that I should take off my armband and we rode on the trolley, in the section reserved for Germans, to the ghetto. At the ghetto gate, we disembarked and proceeded to the hospital. I put the armband back on, out of fear of SS patrols. Schultze ordered my brother and Dr. Bielenki, a prominent Jewish lung specialist, to appear. Bielenki was afraid that Schultze had come to kill Pesach so he reported that he was in excellent condition and would soon be ready to return to work. On the way out, however, he whispered to me in Polish that Pesach was very sick.

As we left the hospital, I asked Schultze to let me stop at the building on Miła Street where my aunt Bela lived with her husband. I saw her briefly and we brought each other up to date on what was happening with each of us.

The last time I heard my brother Pesach's voice was on April 17, 1943. I pleaded with Schultze to let me call him at the Jewish Hospital in the ghetto. Schultze placed the call himself and got Pesach on the phone. Pesach was optimistic. He told me: don't be afraid, everything will be fine, and we'll see each other soon.

The Warsaw ghetto uprising started on *Erev Pesach*, the Eve of Passover, April 19, 1943. The ghetto was surrounded and the battle went into high gear. That morning, I was doing my work, seeing to it that the oven was lit and that the coffee urn was ready for breakfast. I could see a wall of fire and pillars of smoke rising from the ghetto, about nine kilometers from where we were.

While I was working, *Stabsfeldwebel* Iven called me over and complained that what was going on in the ghetto was plain banditry. The Germans had protected and fed the Jews in the ghetto, and this was how they were being repaid: by

110

Jews revolting and killing "our German soldiers." Nobody with a sound mind would kill people who were protecting him. Justice would prevail. The Germans would take care of these bandits. However, I was not to worry. Nothing would happen to me because I was not one of them.

It was difficult for me to listen to this. I knew who those people fighting in the ghetto were, and I knew that they were not bandits. I knew that my brother Pesach was in the fire and he was no bandit. And he knew my brother because Pesach had worked for him before becoming ill. Iven had even sent him to the ghetto hospital. Iven seemed to be asking for my opinion and I was going to give it to him. So I said: "You remember my brother, that decent boy whom you supervised for some months? He is one of the persons you are calling a bandit." He heard me out and walked away.

It was a lovely day, and the ghetto was burning. There was no wind and the smoke went up straight like a pillar, as if God were receiving a sacrifice.

The fire burned for about two weeks. All that time, we worked at the airfield as usual. We got information about what was happening inside the ghetto from Poles working at the airfield, from conversations we overheard between the Germans, and from bulletins posted in the airfield's offices.

We were constantly exposed to abuse but the situation grew particularly tense as the fighting in the ghetto intensified, and the Germans suffered losses of killed and wounded.

At about this time, a German informed Marek Mandeltort, one of my fellow prisoners, that we were being confined to our barracks because the Gestapo had issued orders to move us elsewhere. However, I still had a permit that Iven had given to me, allowing me to walk unescorted between the barracks and the airfield. Sometimes, some of the Jews who worked with me gave me money to buy some food for them at Próchniak's grocery store, which I passed on the way back to the *Fahrkolonne*.

Two days before we were moved from the airfield, Mordechai and Hanoch Glatstein (Mordechai was a rabbinical student at the Tachkemoni School of Religion in Warsaw) gave me twenty zlotys to buy food for them. Later that day, before I had a chance to leave the airfield and get to the grocery, Iven took me aside and said: "I have given the sentry orders to let you pass if you want to walk out of the airfield. There are two roads. One leads to the right, the other to the left. It is up to you. Think it over." The left was in the direction of the barracks and the right was in the direction of Warsaw. His words frightened me very much. I was not sure whether he was playing a game with me and would have me shot if I took him up on the offer or whether he was genuinely giving me a chance to escape. Later I discovered that he really meant it and I could have walked out.

I did not know what to do. Maybe I could escape and save my life. On the other hand, there were great dangers associated with such an attempt. I had no place to go, no money, no one to help me. I also had a feeling of guilt for leaving my people to their fate. I was concerned about the effect of my disappearance on my fellow inmates, although the chances that they would be punished were small. Earlier, some Jews had escaped from our unit without the rest of us being punished. I also kept thinking that perhaps members of my family were still alive in some work camp somewhere and I might meet them there. I knew that these were illusions but I could not free myself from them.

I walked out of the airfield, not knowing whether I would return. My first stop was Próchniak's grocery store. I asked him whether I could make a telephone call and he agreed. I called my friend Naftali Złoto. I had not seen him for over a year but I still remembered his telephone number. It was at an address on the Aryan side where he was living with a gentile woman. (He had been married to a Jewish woman in the ghetto but she had been caught in an action and deported.) A woman answered the phone and I asked for Antoni, his new name which I myself had forged on his ID card. He was not home so I left my number for him to call back which he did very quickly. I told him that I was in a bad situation, that I could not get to him and asked him to come to meet me at the address I gave him. He agreed but said it would take at least an hour. While I was waiting, Próchniak's daughter played Madame Butterfly on the piano. The music blended with the turmoil and confusion that filled me.

In about an hour, Naftali arrived dressed as a German, in a Tyrolean hat with a feather, a leather coat, and boots. I asked him what to do: should I escape or go back to the barracks? He advised me to escape and was willing to put me up in his house for the first night. After that, we would see. He offered me one hundred zlotys and a gun. He said he had another gun for himself, which he would use to take his own life if necessary. I did not accept the gun but I finally agreed to take the money. I told him that I would make up my mind about escaping by the following day. Meanwhile, I would return to the barrack. We kissed each other and he left.

I bought the potatoes for the Glatsteins, and with Naftali's money, bought some food to share with the others. I slipped the twenty zlotys I had left into a slit in my shirt collar.

It was not easy to reject Iven's offer of escape and return to the barracks. But, in the end, I decided to go where the other Jews were going. I had to share their fate.

Concentration Camps and Death Camps during the Nazi Era

(Polish borders until September 1, 1939)

Estonia

Sweden

Baltic Sea

Latvia

Lithuania

Gdańsk (Danzig)

Rostock

Stutthof

East Prussia

Wilno

Mińsk

Germany

Stettin

Niemen

Poland

Sachsenhausen
Oranienburg

Oder

Poznań

Vistula

Treblinka

Berlin

Warta

Chelmno

Warsaw

Bug

Brześć

Prypeć

Leipzig

Łódź

Dresden

Zschachwitz

Breslau
Wrocław

Radom

Sobibór

Lublin

Trawniki

Pilica

Poniatowa

Majdanek

Leitmeritz
Theresienstadt

Budzyń

Prague

Kraśnik

Cracow

Płaszów

Bełżec

Flossenbürg

Czechoslovakia

Auschwitz

Wieliczka

Żółkiew

Janowski

Lwów

USSR

Vienna

Austria

Budapest

Hungary

Rumania

● Cities

○ Towns

Concentration Camps

Death Camps

0   100 km

12

It was early on the morning of May 9, 1943, a beautiful, sunny Sunday morning. Warsaw was quiet. Eighty-nine Jews were assembled in front of the barracks near the Okęcie airport. (Thirteen others had escaped during our last few days at the airfield when word got around that we would be deported. Among them was Licht, the Jew in charge of the Jewish prisoners at the airfield. I met him after the war in Łódź.) We carried some small bundles which we had been permitted to bring. But, since we were afraid that these might be taken away from us, we wore as much clothing as possible, including winter coats, to make certain that we would at least remain with something to wear.

We were surrounded by a platoon of *Luftwaffe* soldiers led by *Feldwebel* Marks to be taken to the *Umschlagplatz*. They led us to the main highway where we were stuffed into trolley cars together with the *Luftwaffe* guards. A truck with more guards followed us. After a ride of about twenty minutes, the trolley stopped near the Żelazna Street gate of the ghetto, which was adjacent to the *Transferstelle,* the offices of the SS and Gestapo that dealt with the affairs of the ghetto and the resettlement activities.

As soon as we entered the ghetto, we were surrounded by a group of *Waffen* SS in full battle gear. They marched alongside our *Luftwaffe* escort taking us to the *Umschlagplatz.* The *Luftwaffe* group escorting us did not leave us yet, because they had to obtain a receipt certifying that they had "returned" us to the SS, from whom we were on loan.

I never understood why they did not take us directly to the *Umschlagplatz* by way of the Aryan sector. It may be that they wanted to march us through the ghetto in order to break our spirits.

We entered Żelazna Street, marching in rows of five, arms linked, with the outside person forced to keep his hands in his pocket because the Germans were afraid of resistance. The ghetto was silent, destroyed. I could hear only occasional gunfire. Many houses had been dynamited and were piles of rubble. Others were still standing as burned-out shells, some still in flames, others just smoldering.

Marching on Smocza Street, crossing Nowolipie Street, then Nowolipki Street, we began to notice with horror small groups of wounded Jews—men, women, and children— many covered with blood, lying and moaning with pain, surrounded by Ukrainian guards. They had been forced out of the bunkers, in which they had been hiding, by the fires. We saw that these people were worse off than we were. Decaying corpses lay around the streets.

I glanced to my right in the direction of 32 Dzielna Street where I had been born. The building was a burned-out shell. As for the Saint Augustine Church across the street, only one of its two towers remained standing. As we marched further, we crossed Pawia Street where I had lived. My house, Number 48, was burned out, as were all the other houses on the street.

When we arrived at the *Umschlagplatz,* we were lined up against a wall. *Feldwebel* Marks presented papers to the SS authorities who signed a receipt for us. As the *Luftwaffe* personnel were about to leave, their eyes met ours. These were people with whom we had worked for about two years. Some degree of personal contact had been established with many of them during the course of our work. There was a degree of bewilderment in their eyes. Then they turned around and left.

The buildings at the *Umschlagplatz* were filled with masses of Jews who looked out of the windows at us. Their eyes had a look of death in them since they had been kept in these buildings for days waiting for their trains. By this time, the number of Jews being captured each day was not very high so people had to wait—sometimes for days—until enough were assembled to fill a transport. Earlier, the mass deportations had sent out thousands each day.

Our group was approached by *Obersturmfuehrer* Brandt, the well-known murderer in charge of all operations in the ghetto, including the transports to the death camps. He was known for his sadism: he would often "drop in" for surprise visits to the ghetto in his open Panzer car. At the sound of the car's powerful motor, people would scatter, trying to hide. He enjoyed target practice, shooting Jews at random from his post in the back seat of the car. Anyone who did not take cover quickly enough was shot.

Brandt spotted Chiel Rinde, a Jew from Berlin who had been assigned by the *Judenrat* to serve as a translator for the Warsaw Gestapo, translating from Hebrew to German. Rinde

Umschlagplatz, Warsaw 1945, after the author's return.
Photo taken by Jan Roguski, a classmate of the author
at the graphic arts school in Warsaw

was standing next to me. Brandt, who knew him, asked: "Rinde, what are you doing here?" Rinde told him that he was being transferred and asked him where we were we going. Brandt answered that we need not worry, we were being sent to Radom to work. He waved *"Auf Wiedersehen"* (So long) and turned away.

Before being pushed into the *Umschlagplatz*, we were all searched for valuables. I saw Ukrainians and SS men beating individuals mercilessly. Men and women were often subjected to degrading searches of their genitals, sometimes with bayonets. The SS laid open valises in front of us and ordered us, under threat of death, to put all our valuables in them. Whatever they confiscated was supposed to go to the Reich, but the SS and Ukrainians pocketed many things for themselves.

I did not give up my few remaining possessions. I still had the twenty zlotys that my friend Naftali Złoto had given me, hidden inside my shirt collar. I held onto my drafting set and a pair of *tfillin*. My drafting set was my means of survival through work. My *tfillin* were the symbol of my faith. I had two watches: Pesach's Bar-Mitzvah watch, and Josef Dov Flamm's pocket watch. I also carried three small photographs of my family, pasted in a little red cardboard folder I had found discarded at the airfield. These were the photographs of my father, my mother, and the one of me with my brothers and sister taken by my father's friend, Bronisław Bykowski, who had pawned his own wedding rings to help pay for my education. Finally, I had my father's tiny razor. These possessions were important to me. I wore them over my heart under my coat. I was not going to give them up. I simply took a chance.

It was a big risk. The Germans didn't want us to have anything that could strengthen us, incite us to rebellion, remind us that we were human. They wanted to detach us from any sense of belonging to a group, of having anything to do with a normal life. Photographs and personal documents were like weapons against them. They became vicious when they found you with such items. It was even worse than discovering that you were hiding gold. If they found photographs on you, you could be shot.

The search process lasted around four or five hours. Then, suddenly, we were being beaten from all sides by the Ukrainians and the SS, who kept screaming and cursing at us. They pushed us into the building that led to the tracks. Then they pushed us, together with the people who had been in the building for days, toward the waiting train, a long one, with maybe fifty freight cars. The platform was a scene of bedlam. The noise was terrible. All the guards—Germans, Ukrainians, Lithuanians, and Latvians—were shouting. They surrounded us and pushed us into the cars. They beat us with whips, canes, and pipes. They grabbed people by the neck with the bent ends of their canes. All this took place very quickly, in an atmosphere of panic. During the loading, many persons were shot, mostly the disabled ones, and their bodies were carried away on two-wheeled carts by Jewish burial details.

I was running, under blows, to the freight cars. As I neared the cars, a Ukrainian guard noticed something bulging in my coat. With his bayonet, he ripped my coat open. In that split second, I lost my *tfillin* and my drafting set.

The next thing I knew, I was inside one of the cattle cars. Our group from the airfield tried to stay together, and most of us ended up in the same car, brothers sharing a common destiny: Mordechai and Hanoch Glatstein, David Grynberg, Adam and Peretz Goldman, Mayer Lachman, George Topas, Chiel Rinde. Other Jews were shoved inside along with us. There were more than one hundred men stuffed into our car. It was so crowded that no one could sit. Once we were in the car we felt a sense of relief because we were not being beaten and screamed at anymore and we felt protected. The doors were shut immediately after the car was full. Those near the windows, which were covered with barbed wire, could look out but we were warned not to do so.

It took about three hours before the train started moving. The atmosphere was tense. Ukrainians standing on top of the cars continued to scream and to shoot sporadically but we did not know whom they were aiming at. The main topic of conversation was our destination. People hoped—wanted to believe—that they were being taken to labor camps. This was particularly true of our group because we had worked at the airfield for about two years now and therefore had diverse experience.

Finally the train began to move, but then it stopped again, at the Gdański Terminal. Here it stood about an hour and a half. The heat had become unbearable because most of us were wearing several layers of clothing, several pairs of underwear, heavy winter coats. We started screaming through the windows, begging for water. The Ukrainians guarding us brought us water only in return for valuables. After receiving them, many guards simply splashed the water into the faces of the victims, cursing and laughing sadistically. But some Polish railroad workers near the tracks did bring a little water, sometimes for money, sometimes for nothing, always taking a risk, because approaching the train was like approaching a fireball. Often, when a person in the car received some water, those around him tried to grab some from him; it often spilled on the floor.

Finally the train began to move. As people realized that the train was moving east rather than south to Radom, where Brandt had said we were going, panic set in. Some began to plan how to break out of the car with the help of saws and knives that they had managed to sneak aboard. But the majority was against such attempts because they believed that those remaining would be killed. Several people were physically stopped from attempting to escape. This debate raged for a while, and then a deadly silence fell. No one escaped from my car.

People had to perform their bodily functions right in the car and gradually the stench became unbearable. The fear of the unknown, however, completely eclipsed the stench and after a while I did not notice it any more. Those of us who had worked at the airfield were in relatively good physical condition but those who had come from the ghetto were in very poor shape. Some people fainted, many were near death. For the entire time I was in the car, I received no food or water, nor did I sit down for a moment. I do not remember feeling thirsty or hungry. I did not react to anything around me. I lost all sense of fear. About midnight, Rabbi Mordechai Glatstein, called out: "Jews, let us say *Viddui*" (the confession recited before death). We all joined him in reciting the prayers. (Rabbi Glatstein and his brother survived the war and settled in the United States.)

The train came to a stop. It was pitch dark. We heard orders barked out in German, Polish, and Ukrainian. We heard the sound of railroad cars being detached and reattached. We had no idea what this meant. After about a half hour, we began to roll in a new direction. We traveled for approximately four hours. Finally, the train came to a halt at dawn. On an adjoining track we observed another train consisting of freight cars, guarded by Ukrainians. Between the two trains there were two tall piles, one of naked corpses, one of clothing. In the cars of the other train we saw naked people and heard voices moaning and begging for mercy. We saw a naked man pry his way out of the window of one of the cars, jump very quickly to the ground and start crawling under the cars. One of the Ukrainians ran after him and killed him with one shot. This occurrence paralyzed us completely.

After another half hour, we heard a commotion around our train. We were surrounded by SS and the doors of the cars were opened, one by one. We heard screams: "*Raus!*" (Out!) We were ordered to jump out of the car, form a single line and run at high speed past two columns of SS who beat us mercilessly. While we ran, a selection was taking place. Individuals were pulled out of the lines of running men and disappeared. We were so terrified we could not even look back to see what was happening. After passing this gauntlet, we were told to line up. I found myself among hundreds of prisoners standing in a U-shaped formation, five rows deep, in a large field facing a row of barracks. Suddenly we were surrounded by Jews in striped uniforms with armbands that said "Kapo." We asked very quietly where we were and they replied: "You are the lucky ones. You will live. You will get water soon." We asked where the others were. They answered: "Don't ask."

The Kapos brought out large metal containers of water, handed out metal bowls, and gave us water. This was the first water we had in over twenty-four hours. Within a half hour, everyone had had a drink. No one pushed or shoved for the water because we were too terrified. A number of high-ranking SS officers came out and one of them addressed us in German. He said that we were in a labor camp and would have to conform to the strict regulations of the camp. The first step was to hand over any valuables we may have on our persons. Anyone found hiding valuables would be shot immediately. They set down a number of open valises on the ground for the valuables and quite a few people dropped in money, jewelry, and other possessions.

Another high-ranking officer appeared riding a horse. All the others treated him with great respect and stood at attention. One of the officers asked those having trades to step forward, and some did. After some hesitation, I stepped forward and told them that I was a *Kunstmahler.* My previous experience had convinced me that the Germans made use of artists. This time it did not work. He screamed at me that they had no need for artists. One of the SS men hit me over the head with a whip and ordered me to step back into the line. One of our former group leaders, Moshe Kessel, who had been Licht's assistant at Okęcie, stepped forward and explained that we were a group of workers who had been employed at the airfield and that we all had experience with airplanes.

This first lineup lasted about an hour and a half. About 150 of us were selected from the entire group of newcomers and led by Kapos into a barrack that already housed several hundred prisoners. These were wooden buildings much like stables. Everywhere there were three levels of bunks with four persons occupying each section of a bunk. The people in each section had to lie on their sides because there was not enough space for four persons lying on their back. To the right of the entrance, there was a small enclosure with two beds for the barrack eldest and his assistant. The barrack held about four hundred persons. Within a short period of time, everyone managed to find places for themselves. The old-timers wanted to know what was going on in the outside world, specifically about the uprising in Warsaw, and the new-comers wanted to know what was to be expected in this camp. We discovered that about ten percent of the old-timers were gentiles, all the others were Jews, mostly from small villages around Lublin. They all wore striped clothing.

We were told by the Kapos that we were in a suburb of Lublin, where my father Chaim Boruch was born. We were outside the death camp of Majdanek, in a "transit" camp. Prisoners in this camp generally were not put to work in Majdanek itself, as this camp served as a distribution center for three subcamps of Majdanek: Trawniki, Poniatowa, and Budzyń. These subcamps had been established to attract volunteers mainly from the Warsaw ghetto shops who had been promised excellent conditions for them and their families if they voluntarily agreed to resettle in these camps. Some people even volunteered.

We received lunch: some warm liquid with some rotten stuff in it. While we were standing around outside the barrack, eating, I met a number of people I knew from Warsaw. They had arrived at Majdanek two weeks earlier. Among them was Yankel Flasterstein, whose father, the grocery-store owner, had helped us in the ghetto, and Leib Drajer, my uncle Avraham Mendel's brother. Drajer told me that, during the uprising, he had seen my brother Pesach on Gęsia Street as the fighting began. This was the first I had heard about my brother since I last spoke with him by telephone on April 17. Exactly what happened to him after that remains an open question. I don't know whether he was involved in the fighting. Or if he was in the hospital on Gęsia Street when it was set on fire and all the patients burned alive. I will never know. All I know is that he died during the uprising in the Warsaw ghetto. He was born during Pesach (Passover), he was named Pesach, and he died during Pesach.

We did nothing that day, May 11, 1943. I studied the fences and the security system that surrounded the camp. This kind of environment was new to me. It seemed easy to escape but I kept these thoughts to myself. I soon learned, however, that the camp was surrounded by mine fields, vicious dogs, and other devices that made escape very difficult. And even if you got out, you would be caught because the surrounding villages were hostile. I felt trapped.

About noon on May 11, a group of Ukrainians headed by *Zugwachman* (Platoon Leader) Bizewski, arrived. There was another selection and about 150 were chosen, including me. We were surrounded by Ukrainians and marched to a waiting train, consisting of a locomotive and two freight cars. At about 3:00 P.M. we were loaded into the cars. During the trip, two Ukrainians at a time would enter the car and demand valuables. They approached each person individually, warning that if we told anyone about this, they would kill us later. To underscore their point, they beat people mercilessly, though they did not kill anyone. I gave one of them my last 20 zlotys, which I had kept hidden in my collar.

The trip took about two hours. The train stopped at a siding in a young forest. We were ordered to get off the train and line up in rows of five. We were marched through the forest on a dirt road that led to a paved road, where we were ordered to march in step. After some minutes, I noticed groups of people being escorted from other directions. I began to hear a melody echoing between the trees. At first, I could not make out the words, but they gradually became clearer: it was a Hassidic melody, "*Yismechu bemalkhuskho*" (Rejoice in Your Kingdom).

All the groups converged on a camp. I observed barbed wire, a gate, and barracks similar to those in Majdanek. Over the gate to the camp was a wooden sign: *Jedem Das Seine* (To Each His Own). We had arrived in Budzyń.

13

We were marched to the rear of the camp and lined up with the rest of the prisoners, about three thousand persons. Standing with the Germans at the *Appellplatz,* the large parade ground where all the lineups were held, were a number of persons in Polish military uniforms wearing high boots and carrying whips. They turned out to be company heads, foremen, and Kapos. These were Jewish POWs who were put to work to prepare the camps and were responsible for camp discipline. The Germans selected them because of their military background. Standing among them was a very handsome, towering man in a Polish officer's uniform with all insignias removed, who was talking to and receiving orders from the Germans. We later learned that he was *Lageraelteste* Noah Stockman, the Jewish leader of the prisoners.

There was total silence, with the three thousand people standing there. We heard the command: "Caps off, look right!" A group of Germans and Ukrainians marched up led by a blond, handsome man in his early thirties, in a well-tailored uniform, with something like a camera hanging from his shoulder. This was Reinhold Feix, the commandant of Budzyń. What looked like a camera was, in fact, an automatic pistol with a fancy butt made of wood inlaid with mother-of-pearl.

Those of us who had just arrived were ordered to run in a circle at high speed and, while doing so, take off all extra clothing, including overcoats, which many of us were still wearing. They had to be piled in the middle. While we did so, we heard a shot from the fancy pistol. An old man was killed.

After the killing, you could feel a certain relief come over the *Appellplatz*. It was as though people hoped that maybe the worst had passed and things would be better for a while. The feeling was that a sacrifice had been offered and the angel of death had been appeased.

At this point, in a very fine and relaxed tone, Feix delivered a speech. He called us his children. We were in a work camp where we would learn how to lead a decent life, provided we obeyed the rules of the camp and submitted to discipline. The old man had been an "old shit" who appeared to him a useless human being. Anyone who didn't hand over his valuables would meet his fate.

(I found out later that Feix had shot and killed the renowned physician and humanitarian, Doctor S. Pupko, in much the same way as the old man. Pupko had arrived in Budzyń in April, 1943, with a transport of eight hundred Jews from the Warsaw ghetto. A friend, who had arrived in that same transport, had witnessed the killing.)

The Kapos laid open valises in front of us and started yelling: "Hand it over. He means it. This is no game." This was said in Yiddish, which Feix understood and enjoyed. In spite of the threats, I kept my treasures: my photographs, my father's razor, and the two watches. I did not feel like giving them up.

The camp was dismissed. The veteran prisoners went to receive their evening food, while we, the new arrivals, were pushed into a barrack. Standing in front of the barrack was a child who looked about six or seven years old. He was dressed in a child-sized SS uniform but I could tell he was a Jew. In Yiddish, he said to me: "If you have something, give it to me." I gave him the two watches and the photographs of my family and pleaded with him to return them to me later. He didn't say anything but the next day he did give them back. Later I learned that he was Feix's mascot. Feix had captured him in a raid on a nearby town. His nicknames were *"Malpe"* (Ape) and "Borscht."

We were made to sit on benches, and barbers using hand clippers cut off all our hair, including the hair of the head and the genital area. We were then led to another part of the barrack where we were supposed to take showers. But first, they poured some disinfecting liquid into our hands and ordered us to rub it all over our bodies. We had to keep it on our bodies for a while and this made our skin burn. People with open wounds suffered terribly. The showers were a relief.

We were then driven to another barrack where we received our clothing. They gave us a shirt, a pair of pants, a jacket, and wooden clogs. No socks. After this, we were force-marched to the kitchen barrack and were told that we would not receive any food because we had not earned it yet. I had not eaten anything for almost three days. To earn our food, we were to spend the whole night washing potatoes and doing other chores in the kitchen. The kitchen was under the supervision of former Jewish military prisoners who were per-

Feix and his mascot, "Borscht"
Budzyń, 1943

mitted to wear their uniforms, without insignias. Most of them were Jews from eastern Poland whom I learned to love. After a while, when the Germans and the Ukrainians left, they gave us as much food as they could.

About 4 A.M., Jewish Kapos drove us out of the kitchen barrack and into Barrack No. 5 which faced the main gate. The left side of the barrack was reserved for us. We were so tired that we fell asleep in no time at all. At 5:45 A.M., we were awakened by the sound of a gong, reinforced by screams of the barrack elders and Kapos. The doors of the barrack were opened and a hot liquid that was supposed to pass for coffee was delivered.

Our group of new prisoners was lined up and counted. They took down our names and trades, and painted large red X's on the backs of our jackets and in the front of the left leg of our pants in order to mark us as prisoners. Then we were assigned to work groups. I was assigned to a group of about thirty or forty prisoners digging ditches alongside the barbed wire fence.

From an area beyond the fence, we smelled a terrible odor. The area had high grass growing in spots, the soil was black and there were mounds everywhere. Circling above this area were large numbers of black crows making loud noises. Later I learned that this area contained the bodies of about two thousand Jews from the adjacent towns murdered by Feix and Handtke, his assistant, several months before my arrival.

The typical day in Budzyń started with a wakeup gong at 6:00 A.M., a quick visit to the latrine, and a quick washing. The latrine consisted of a long building with two parallel ditches. Every few feet, crossed logs had been placed over the ditch on which we had to sit while relieving ourselves. They did not give us toilet paper. Some used leaves, others had bits of paper, while still others had nothing at all with which to wipe themselves. The whole camp, some three thousand prisoners, was given approximately ten to fifteen minutes to use the latrines. The latrine only accommodated fifty, sixty people at a time. There wasn't enough time for everyone to use it. People were sick with diarrhea, cramps, and couldn't finish that quickly. Many prisoners suffered from dysentery and were soiling themselves all the time. The odor in the latrine was unbearable. After the visit to the latrine, we had to wash. There were two long wooden tubs, like troughs, with pipes running across them in which there were faucets. The crush to get at the faucets was terrible.

After the washing, warm liquid that was supposed to resemble coffee but was really made with chicory was distributed in the barracks. We had about half an hour for the visit to the latrine, the washing, and drinking this warm liquid. Then we had to run to the lineup.

The camp was divided into companies of one hundred prisoners each. Each company was divided into ten groups of ten persons. Everyone had his place in the lineup. One of the prisoners was a foreman who was responsible for the other nine. After the company leader reported the presence of one hundred prisoners, they were counted by an SS man to determine whether the report was correct. Sick prisoners and those who had died during the night usually had to be dragged to the lineup and placed in front of the assembled company. Often the Kapos, accompanied by the SS and Ukrainians, would enter the barracks to check on the sick and the dead.

If everything went smoothly, the lineup would take about half an hour. But often there were complications—the numbers seemed never to add up—and the lineup took longer. While the life of a Jew didn't matter at all, the count did. The numbers had to be precisely correct as if every Jew was a precious commodity.

Almost at every lineup there was beating or killing. The worst incidents took place during the evening lineup. Sometimes, there were alleged infractions of the rules, such as finding potatoes on a prisoner, or a spoon, which was considered a weapon. At other times, people were beaten or killed without any pretense of a reason. Feix would ride into the camp on his white horse. On a number of occasions, he would throw the reins of his horse around the neck of a prisoner and make the horse rear, thereby strangling the victim. Sometimes he released the reins before the prisoner was dead, leaving him in agony. At other times, he rode into the camp on his motorcycle, whipping people while they jumped out of his way. He would order his dog Rolph, a German shepherd, to attack prisoners at his command, ripping out their genitals or flesh from other parts of their bodies. One of those attacked was my friend Mayer Lachman. Mayer and I had met while working at the airfield in Warsaw. He was a barber who was assigned to cut prisoners' hair in Budzyń. He had guts, though, and before long he was promoted to cutting the hair of the German and Ukrainian camp personnel. He was often rewarded for his work with a cigarette or a piece of bread. In the camps, these extra bits of food or cigarettes were lifesavers. Mayer was a *"mensch,"* an extraordinary human being who always shared these "profits" with his fellow prisoners, thus prolonging their lives. One day Feix ordered him to stand by the wall of the barrack, and commanded his dog: *"Mensch, beiss den Hund!"* (Man, bite the dog!) Rolph ripped out a chunk of Mayer's inner thigh. Then Feix allowed him to be taken to the infirmary, where they sewed him together. Mayer survived this attack. (After the

SS Untersturmführer Feix
Budzyń, 1943

war, he required surgery to repair the damage. He now lives in New York with his wife and family.)

The main purpose of Budzyń was to supply workers for industrial plants located near the camp. These were prewar munitions and armament factories that had been taken over by a number of German organizations. The most important was the Heinkel Werke, which repaired airplane parts. There was also the Todt organization that repaired tanks and other heavy equipment, and other, smaller industrial operations. Budzyń supplied workers for all these enterprises. The march to these workplaces took about forty-five minutes to an hour.

Work began at approximately eight o'clock in the morning and continued until noon. For lunch, we received some soup brought from the camp kitchen in Budzyń by prisoners supervised by Ukrainians. This was a thin mixture of water flavored with black salt, containing a few pieces of potatoes or cabbage, some leaves, and whatever other rotten substances they could find. While we were drinking this soup outdoors, the German supervisors had their lunch in the mess room, though some of them went home to eat. The lunch period lasted from half an hour to an hour, depending on how busy we were. Occasionally, if a German took a liking to a particular Jew, because of some special service the Jew had performed for him or his wife or girlfriend or—and this was even more rare—out of pity, he might bring him something from his lunch. Theoretically, a German could get into trouble for such an action but I know of no one who actually did. Nevertheless, when a German gave food to a Jew, he always instructed him to hide it.

Work resumed after lunch and continued until five o'clock. Compared to staying in camp, work was a relief. So when the time for stopping work approached, a deep anxiety began to spread. Before leaving the industrial complex, the groups were counted by the SS and if the numbers did not come out right, an alert would be sounded and we were not allowed to leave. There were occasions when we were kept in the work complex for hours under heavy guard, sometimes until midnight or later, before we were allowed to return to the camp. But normally, we would be back in the camp by about six o'clock.

There would be another lineup, often followed by speeches designed to educate us. If Feix was in a good mood, he would order us to sing. The Ukrainians would march around watching our mouths carefully: anyone who wasn't singing properly was beaten viciously because not singing indicated dissatisfaction with the camp. The song Feix requested most frequently was "Marianna," a popular Polish tango. He also enjoyed Jewish songs. He had gotten to know the names of some of them and would order particular ones to be sung. He especially liked Hassidic music, most of all *Yismechu!* (Rejoice!) After such a performance, we could hope for a peaceful evening.

Singing was also often ordered after killings. A victim would be paraded in front of the camp, and his crime announced. This could be anything from stealing a potato, to having an appearance that Feix did not like, to planning to escape. The victim was then made to kneel and was executed by a shot in the head, usually by Feix or his assistant Otto, a Ukrainian platoon leader. Once, soon after our arrival, four Jewish POWs accused of planning to escape were killed in this way, some twenty-five feet from where I stood. After such murders, Feix would speak, justifying the killing and holding it up as an example for the rest of us. Then we were often ordered to sing, as if to say: the wicked person has been punished and the good prisoners will learn a lesson from this justified punishment.

After the evening lineup was completed, and if the numbers were found correct, the groups were marched to the kitchen barrack and dinner was distributed. This usually consisted of another thin soup. If you were lucky, or the prisoner distributing the soup liked you, he gave you slightly thicker soup from the bottom of the pot where more of the solid stuff accumulated.

To eat your soup, you were issued some kind of *schissel*, a banged-up metal bowl, or a cup. Sometimes you got both. There was nothing uniform about these utensils. You got whatever they had on hand. You punched a hole in it and tied it on you with a wire or a string. The bowl was a treasure. If you lost it, you had no way to eat, and had to scrounge around for an empty tin from conserves, discarded from the German mess hall. You broke off its lid and used that as your bowl.

At dinner, they usually added a piece of bread to the portion of soup. Calling this substance "bread" is itself an exaggeration. No bakery could pass this off as bread. It was dark, made of sawdust mixed with flour. Nevertheless, this stuff was terribly important to us. Kapos took the loaves of bread to the barracks, where they cut them and distributed the slices to the prisoners. The cutting of the slices was a ritual. It was essential that the slices be equal because people's lives depended on it. Most Kapos tried their best to make the slices equal. Occasionally there were bitter fights over food. This was particularly the case when a prisoner was too weak to eat his portion and there were many hungry people who wanted it. People fought over pieces of bread, which were often no more than torn, dirty scraps by the time the victors secured them. Every little bit was devoured, no matter how dirty. It was a mad scene.

Most persons ate their bread as soon as they received it

because it could be stolen if not eaten immediately. Nevertheless, some persons kept a part of their bread for the morning.

On Sundays, and sometimes—rarely—during the week, we also received a spoonful of marmalade or margarine.

After supper, we had from one-and-a-half to two hours of leisure time. During this time, we either sat around in the barrack or walked around outside to discuss the events of the day. We exchanged information, rumors we had heard, conversations we had overheard, reports about how the war was going, what was happening in other camps. Some Jews recited their evening prayers. At nine o'clock the lights went out. Shoes had to be lined up in front of the sleeping bunks and we crawled to our places to sleep.

In the midst of this misery, there was an occasional demand by the SS officers for music and drama. They claimed it would "lift our morale." Of course, they were bored and wanted some entertainment. In my barrack, Barrack 5, there were a few actors from Warsaw, among them Moshe Cohen, and two musicians, Sasha Bulkowstein, an accordionist, and Stanley Flato, a violinist whose family I had known from home. Flato would play the violin, standing barefoot, his feet swollen from starvation. Later, the camp leadership gave him some shoes to fit his feet, and even allowed him to hold on to the violin (stolen from the Jewish population, homes like my own), in case the Germans suddenly got an urge for music.

At other times, the Germans requested theater. I remember once quickly sketching a "shtetl" on an old sheet and against this backdrop, Moshe, Sasha, and Stanley performed some scenes from Sholom Aleichem, in Yiddish. Our honored guests, the SS officers, occupied the "orchestra seats" and laughed wildly throughout the performance. We knew they were ridiculing us, but at least it calmed the beasts and

An evening of music
Budzyń, 1943

we could hope for a quiet night. Because the chances for a quiet night were not great.

The Ukrainian guards occasionally "dropped in" during the night, demanding that Flato play a *czardas,* some gypsy music, or some Ukrainian folk tunes, their favorite. But, more often, they were not there for the culture. They came in, frequently drunk, to rob us of whatever we had left, and to beat us. The beatings were terrible. They did these things on their own, without the knowledge of the Germans. In fact, they always threatened to kill their victims if the Germans were told about the attacks. At times, they would negotiate for a ransom with the barrack elder and if a deal could be worked out, the attack was avoided. At other times, they did not feel like negotiating but preferred to beat. Such attacks also occurred in the women's barracks for sexual purposes. Rapes committed against women and young girls were supposed to be kept secret, especially because sexual acts with Jews were considered *Rassen Schande,* desecration of the pure race, and were therefore punishable offenses. However, these acts were often committed in the barracks and silently witnessed by other women prisoners. We heard about these attacks from relatives—fathers, brothers—and from prison doctors who silently treated the victims.

We worked six days a week. Sunday was supposed to be a day off. Officially we were only required to clean all our so-called belongings, all our rags, and straighten the straw we slept on, when we had it. Whether we had straw or not depended on Feix's mood. If he was in a good mood, he might order fresh straw from the local peasants so we would have "good beds to sleep on." At other times, he made us burn the straw, claiming that it was too lice-infested or the threat of contagious disease was too great.

On Sunday he often ordered us to clear a young forest,

without any tools. We would work for several hours, ripping out young trees with our bare hands, while guards stood over us, beating us the whole time. Under these conditions, people collapsed, some from heart attacks, others with severe injuries to their hands. Feix would ride into the area on his horse to check what was happening, bringing along some police dogs, especially his favorite, Rolph. If someone's work did not please him, he shot him on the spot. Then his bloodthirst was satisfied. He would have us clear the area, bury the dead, pick up the wounded, and march back to camp. Sunday fun was over.

14

In Budzyń there were various kinds of Jews. The earliest inmates were Jews from the surrounding Lublin region who had been brought in 1941 to build the camp. The largest single group of these came from Kraśnik, a town seven kilometers away. Before the war, it had been a well-organized town with many Jewish points of view represented. Most of its Jews were small merchants and artisans with various trades. The majority was observant.

The first shipment of Jews from Warsaw, about eight hundred persons, arrived in Budzyń toward the end of April, 1943, after the beginning of the Warsaw ghetto uprising. Our group of about 150 persons, which arrived on May 12, 1943, was the second Warsaw contingent. The influx of the Warsaw Jews had a significant impact on the camp. Before we arrived, the Jews in Budzyń had heard about the uprising in the Warsaw ghetto. When we appeared, we were seen as heroes. Not only were we considered the sophisticated city Jews, we were witnesses to the electrifying drama of the uprising.

The news of the uprising lifted the morale of the Jews in the camp beyond description. For the first time, Jews were fighting with weapons in hand against the German murderers. This saved Jewish honor. They could not do enough for us. At the same time, our appearance injected a new dimension of terror into the camp. The Germans called us "the Warsaw bandits" and promised to treat us accordingly. This endangered all the Jews because the Germans were not going to distinguish between those from Warsaw and elsewhere.

In these transports were a number of rabbis, physicians, academicians, leaders of various Jewish political groups, and other intellectuals. Among them were Rabbi Stockhammer, Rabbi Ziemba, and Rabbi Posner, the director of the Jewish cemetery in Warsaw. There was Dr. Rubin Tylbor, a physician from Warsaw, with his son Henry; David Grynberg, a Hebrew educator, who had worked with me at Okęcie airfield; S. Falk, a leader of the Bund in Poland; and David Rosenthal, writer and scholar.

We tried to protect these prominent people as much as possible because they were sources of strength for the Jewish community. We kept their identity secret because, had the Germans known who they were, they would have been murdered immediately to destroy all potential Jewish leadership. The rabbis, for example, had shaved off their beards long ago, for fear of reprisals.

Physicians, on the other hand, usually identified themselves to the camp authorities when they arrived, because the SS was looking for doctors to minister to their own medical needs, and because their services were needed by the prisoners. The SS had set up a *revier,* a little infirmary in a barrack with a few beds, staffed by a few doctors and male nurses. As new doctors entered the camp, they were assigned to the hospital. The staff was given limited amounts of medicine and surgical tools with which to treat the sick.

Some of the physicians I knew in Budzyń were Polish Jews who had been captured during the Warsaw ghetto uprising. Others were German Jews who had arrived in earlier transports. Dr. Foerster, the head of the camp hospital, was from Vienna. Dr. Erich Mosbach came from Germany. He was Feix's favorite. After tortures and executions, Dr. Mosbach had to appear in a white coat and a stethoscope to declare the victim officially dead. This was all part of the pretense of order: people were executed according to regulations and then had to be declared dead by a physician.

One of the male nurses was Isak Arbus, an outstanding human being who often risked his own life to help the sick. He was responsible for caring for minor illnesses. Then, typhus broke out in the camp. Some of those who became ill tried to hide in the infirmary, because you could never rest in the barracks, where they were always dragging you in and out, to work and back. The doctors tried to disguise the nature of their illness, claiming that these were cases of flu. But the truth came out when one of the German *Meisters* (supervisors) came down with typhus. Feix was furious and said he would take care of the matter the next day. The infirmary staff quickly sent patients in slightly better shape back to the barracks, thus saving their lives. The next morning, the Germans took the most obviously sick patients, who couldn't move on their own, out behind the camp to be shot. Dr. Foerster, Arbus, and another male nurse, Chajkin, accompanied the group to the execution area. At the last minute, they still managed to pull out a few more people and save them.

In my experience, religious Jews were the best people in

camp. They were the bearers of Eastern European Orthodox tradition as it had been passed down through generations of life in small Jewish communities. I saw them congregating in the morning, praying. They believed that a miracle would save us. Generally speaking, they opposed mutinies or break-outs from the camp because they took seriously the consequences to those remaining. These religious Jews were the most sensitive people in the camp, the most trustworthy. They showed the greatest compassion to their brethren.

The assimilated Jews I came across in Budzyń, the *intelligentsia,* were the least exemplary group in the camp. They were not comfortable with the simple Jews and generally mixed only among themselves. They were the least helpful to others, the least likely to share a piece of bread with a fellow Jew. Very often, these Jews were the first to disintegrate because they could not adjust to the terrifying conditions.

The simple, poor Jews were quite different. They understood misery, having known it their whole lives. As a result, they were more resistant to conditions in the camps. They were also generally compassionate to their fellow Jew. I remember a poor horse-cart driver by the name of Glatstein (not a relative of the rabbi), and a porter, Meyer *Kocioł,* Meyer the Kettle, so-called because he was so round when he first arrived. In the mornings, these two would fight their way to the place where the warm liquid was being distributed to obtain some portions for those who were too weak to get their own. They would encourage them to keep fighting and not give up. Meyer *Kocioł* eventually gave away his soul. He started losing weight, losing strength, and under the fearsome pounding of camp life, he perished.

One of the sources of spiritual support in my group was another Jew who came from the poor. Yehuda Gram, a Jew from Zdzisno in Lithuania, was the son of a horse-cart driver.

But he took after his father who had also been a Talmudic scholar. Before the war, Gram had been a student in a yeshiva. Then he was drafted into the Polish army and captured by the Germans. In the darkest hours of our life in the camp, he supported us by preaching a faith drawn from the Bible and the writings of our sages, especially *Pirkei Avot* (The Ethics of Our Fathers). A man of great wit and charm, Gram knew the prayer book by heart and conducted services in the barrack. He had a beautiful voice. He urged us to have hope, to remember all the miracles that had happened to our people throughout our history. He kept telling us that we would survive, we must survive, that we were not all meant to die. That's what we wanted to believe. Nobody wanted to believe in death. Everyone wanted to believe that he would be the last one.

Yehuda Gram and I developed a relationship like family. He became my camp-brother. We were committed to helping one another, to sharing a good word and a piece of bread. Every bit of support was crucial in helping us get through this time, which was like one long night stretching before our eyes. We clung to each other even when we were transferred from camp to camp later on. (Yehuda Gram survived and established his life in Israel, with his wife, two daughters, and a son. He died in 1990.)

Another group in the camp was the prisoner personnel, the Kapos. They were prisoners themselves, picked by the SS to execute their orders promptly and police the other inmates. Among the Kapos, we found both good and bad people. I did not meet one religious Kapo.

Some Kapos outdid even the Germans at some of their terror tactics. The Germans and their helpers were constantly screaming at us. But one of the scariest screamers was a Kapo nicknamed *Der Geyler Mordche* (redheaded Mordechai) from

Łódź. His screaming actually saved many Jewish lives. The more noise he made, the more fearsome he sounded, the more the Germans were satisfied that he had us well in hand and they could leave us to him. He used to scream at the top of his lungs in Yiddish: "Scream louder! Scream *gevald!* Scream that it hurts!" This amused the Germans so much that they often left his victims alone. He also often took over the task of whipping prisoners from the Germans assigned to carry this out. He made all the right motions, but his strokes didn't fall quite as hard, or with the same precision, and his whip did not have lead tips.

The majority of the Jews in the camp, in spite of everything that they had seen, still did not believe that the German plan was the total destruction of the Jewish people. We still believed that they needed our labor and that this would ensure our survival. I was one of those who, naively, did not draw the proper conclusions from what I saw. The will to survive began to distort our perception of reality.

These were only my impressions. There was hardly any opportunity to discuss these things among ourselves. There was a constant flow of events which didn't let us rest. Only when we were lying on that goddamn bunk at the end of another miserable day, surrounded by pain, could we exchange a few words.

15

After a few days of digging ditches, I was given a new assignment. I had reported that I was an artist and Noah Stockman, the Jewish head of the camp, assigned me to a group of about twenty-five painters responsible for painting the interiors and exteriors of buildings within the *Heinkel Werke,* the Heinkel Works. This unit was called Number 11, because we were housed in Building 11 at the *Werke.* Every day, following the lineup, we were marched to the location where we were to paint that day. We painted walls in various offices and factory buildings in the huge industrial complex. Some of the areas we worked on were the size of hangars. We also painted trucks, wagons, and tanks in camouflage colors.

We were led by Samuel Jarniewski, a Jew from Grodno. He was a very shrewd person who constantly tried to make us seem as useful as possible to the Germans because this was thought to protect the group. When he discovered that I could do German calligraphy, he immediately informed the Germans of this and they took full advantage of my skill. I was often assigned to paint signs, because the Germans insisted on everything being properly identified.

Our unit was under the supervision of a German master painter from Berlin, Karl Jaeger. He was a decent man who praised good work, liked to drink beer and tell stories about his prewar life in Berlin. It was my impression that Jaeger knew what was going on in the camp and did not approve of it, though he could not change it. His decency was revealed in small but important ways.

He had a dog, a Dalmatian. He put one Jew, an older man named Nissenbaum in charge of the dog, and sent word to the mess hall that he should be given a full pail of soup for the dog every day. He never told Nissenbaum what to do with the soup, but he must have known that no dog would eat an entire pail of soup. After giving the dog his due, Nissenbaum used to divide the rest of the soup between himself, his two sons, and some of the rest of us, including me and Jarniewski, the Jewish foreman of the painting unit. So our lives were prolonged for a few more days, thanks to Jaeger and his dog. (Other Jews, who worked as handlers of the attack dogs, also survived thanks to these animals, because they were able to share bits of their food.)

I was still holding onto my brother's "Chronometer" watch, which our uncle Boruch had given him for his bar mitzvah. One day, several weeks after my arrival at Budzyń, we were marching back to camp from the industrial plant. The SS did not always supervise these marches, and the Ukrainian guards often took advantage of their absence to steal whatever they could from us. That day, they grabbed me, the way you snatch a chicken for the slaughter, dragged me inside the guardhouse at the gate and started searching me. They practically undressed me completely. I had taped the watch, just the watch without the strap, in my left armpit. But they lifted my arms and found it. The Ukrainian laughed at me. "You have more luck than brains," he said. "I'm taking it." He warned me to keep my mouth shut about the incident or he would kill me.

I didn't grasp how dangerous it was for me to have concealed the watch, and how lucky I was that they, rather than Feix, had found it. Had Feix discovered it, I could have been shot instantly. My friend, Isak Arbus, the male nurse, paid dearly for his watch. One day, Feix entered the infirmary and noticed that Arbus had a watch. Arbus tried to explain that he was only using it to measure the patients' pulses. Feix said he would shoot him. Doctor Foerster intervened and Feix relented: if Arbus could take fifty lashes, he could live. They stripped Arbus, and Feix began whipping him. When they whipped you, you yourself had to count the strokes out loud. When they got to about twenty-four or so lashes, Arbus lost the count. He said twenty-eight. Feix ordered him to start counting again, from one. By the time they reached about fifty lashes, Arbus was unconscious. They kept whipping him until he had been given the full seventy-five. He almost bled to death. But he survived.

Shortly after this incident, I asked my friend, Szyja Hochrad, the master watch repairman, whether he had come across my watch because the Ukrainians often brought him watches for repair or assessment. He replied, "You mean the small chronometer? Sure! The son-of-a-bitch brought it in to be fixed." I told him it had been my brother's. He warned me to keep quiet and be glad that the Ukrainian took it and not Feix.

I still hung onto the Waltham pocket watch that had belonged to my father's cousin, Flamm. I guess I didn't acknowledge the danger.

I gradually became known around camp as the *Kunstmahler*. About two months after my arrival in Budzyń, I was summoned by a low-ranking SS guard and ordered to do a charcoal drawing of his girlfriend from a photograph. He had first gone to Jacob Eljowicz, a former POW and photographer who ran the photographic studio for the SS. Eljowicz was too busy and sent him to me because I had told him that I was an artist. My foreman, Jarniewski, permitted me to work in the basement of Building 11, which housed a number of shops. I worked on this drawing for three days and the German was very satisfied with the result. He gave me a piece of bread and some cigarettes.

After this, my reputation was established. I was commissioned to do an oil painting of one of the German administrators, Stepan, a naval officer from Rostock. I painted a life-sized, full-color portrait of him in his blue naval uniform, with all his insignia and medals. This took me almost three weeks, working part time. For a number of hours each day I had to do other work but then I would return to the same basement room to work on the painting. He also was very satisfied, and though he did not give me anything for the painting, the fact that he accepted it was a good sign.

My talent became known among the Germans, both the SS guards and the civilian employees. In the autumn of 1943, the SS administration assigned me to decorate the recreation rooms in the German civilian settlement near the camp. Among the things I did was to paint slogans on the wall, such as *Meine Ehre Ist Treue* (My Honor Is Loyalty), rendered in Gothic script. I worked on this project for several weeks.

Occasionally, we were assigned to work in the residential

area where the German supervisors lived. I was ordered to decorate the rooms of children of the civilian employees. In the course of this work, I met at least a dozen different families. The men were at work during the day and came home occasionally for lunch. The women, who were home tending to the house and the children, rarely spoke to me and when they did, would address me as *Kunstmahler.* Occasionally, they gave me some food and permitted me to eat it in the kitchen. One time, Jaeger took me to copy an illustration in a children's book onto the wall of a child's room. After I finished, he invited me to his apartment to join him and his wife for lunch. She served us scrambled eggs, bread, and coffee, and we spoke about art and his prewar life. This was so extraordinary that I did not even tell anybody in the camp about it because I did not want to arouse envy.

In the fall of 1943, the SS officers from Budzyń hosted their peers from the neighboring camps at a private celebration. It was an *Oktoberfest,* but they called it a *Schlachtfest* (slaughter festival). They gathered a number of pigs in a field near their barracks and entertained themselves by shooting them with their pistols, something they found wildly amusing. The field was soaked with the blood of the pigs. Afterwards, Jews were summoned to skin the pigs that the Germans later roasted and ate.

While this was going on, I was ordered to produce erotic drawings on large sheets of paper stretched across frames set up in the SS barracks. They gave me pornographic photographs and drawings to enlarge. I was ordered by one SS commandant to draw a caricature of a fellow officer, whom he did not like, having intercourse with a pig. I did not want to bring out the face too clearly, so I just made a rough sketch, and included some obvious features, including the peaked cap and the rank. They also gave me condoms which I had to blow up like balloons and decorate with pornographic pictures and slogans such as "*Liebe, rauche, saufe bis zum letzten Hauche*" (Love, smoke, and gorge yourself, to the last breath).

The man behind this project was SS *Unterscharfuehrer* Schragner who fancied himself an art expert. He warned me, laughing, that if I did not do a proper job, I would receive a *Bauchschuss*, a shot in the belly. This was a most horrible death, because you would be dying for hours. Naturally, I was terrified. But I tried to be as professional and as collected as I could be, to make a good impression on the beasts. And it was strange: while I was working, I lost all my fear. When I took a pen or a brush into my hand, I felt extremely secure. These were my weapons, my only defense. As long as I was working, they weren't going to come in and beat me. They had to come in and look at what I was doing. Even though I was following their orders, while I worked, they were in *my* territory.

When I was finished, Schragner invited his guests to view the exhibit. They burst into wild laughter which still rings in my ears. They asked who had done these drawings and Schragner motioned in my direction. They exclaimed: "*Fabelhaft!*" (Fabulous!) My reward was a pack of cigarettes, which Schragner threw over his shoulder at me.

Later that night, after we were asleep in our barracks, the lights suddenly went on and I heard voices asking for the *Kunstmahler.* I was certain that I had done something wrong and that this was the end. I jumped down from my shelf and found three SS men waiting for me. They ordered me to run toward the main gate. The searchlights from the watchtowers were on me as I proceeded to the SS casino. Music was blaring and I was confronted with an orgy: men and women, drunk, dancing madly, engaged in wild sexual activity. Many of the high SS officers from the neighboring camps were present. A small military band of German soldiers pumped away on the side. Schragner ordered me to observe a particular table at which an SS officer was embracing a woman. I was to produce a caricature of this scene and have it ready by the time of the lineup in the morning. I told him that I had no materials to do the job. He replied that I could use his office where I would find everything necessary.

After I finished the caricature during the night, I was not allowed to return to the camp because to do so would have awakened everybody and created a disturbance. I therefore remained in the office until the morning, deeply anxious about how my drawing would be received. I was returned to the camp about the time of the lineup, carrying the drawing with me. As the lineup began, Schragner appeared and demanded the drawing. I handed it to him, he glanced at it quickly and seemed satisfied. I was greatly relieved when I was ordered back into the ranks. Though I had not slept most of the night, I had to work that day as if nothing had happened.

Needless to say, the other prisoners thought that I would not return when they saw me called out during the night. When I reappeared, the surprise was great. Being called out to spend a night with the Germans for interrogation was cause for suspicion, especially if one reappeared uninjured. But over time, my fellow inmates had developed confidence in me. I explained what had happened and they believed me.

At various times, because of my work as an artist, I was able to request the assistance of various prisoners and thereby save them from selections that would probably have led to their deaths. One such case was Itzhak Dorfsman, who was about to be taken away to the gas chambers. At the last minute, I persuaded *Unterscharfuehrer* Klauss to release him so he could work with me. He said, "You can have the dog if you need him."

On one occasion, units of troops returning from the

Eastern front passed through our area. They visited the factory complex and made friends with the German supervisors. Jaeger told them about me and ordered me to paint a number of scenes of the local countryside as gifts for these soldiers. They particularly liked Polish village scenes. I had to produce quantities of these paintings so I lined up about ten wooden boards at a time and began mass production. I first painted all the skies, then all the trees, then all the Polish village wells, and so on. I made sure to vary them slightly so that each one would be unique. I even signed them.

At the time, I was wearing my wooden clogs and decided to exploit this new situation to obtain a decent pair of boots. When a young German soldier who seemed more decent than the others asked for a painting, I pointed at my clogs and asked him whether he could obtain a pair of leather shoes in exchange for them. He replied that he could not do that (what would he do with wooden clogs?) but if I obtained any old pair of leather shoes, he could trade them for new ones. I went to the camp clothing warehouse and told the Jew in charge that the wooden shoes hurt my feet terribly. He took pity on me and gave me a pair of old leather shoes from a dead Jew. Next morning, my German client appeared with an almost new pair of military boots in excellent condition. I gave him the old pair of shoes and rewarded him with two of my masterpieces. I immediately made the boots appear worn by pouring all kinds of garbage on them because to appear in German military boots could easily lead to one's death. These boots saved my life during the coming winters. I was liberated in them.

16

One day in the beginning of autumn, 1943, at about three in the afternoon, we were working in the industrial complex when we were ordered to stop work and line up immediately. One could feel disaster in the air. Whenever work stopped before the usual 5:00 P.M. quitting time, we could expect something terrible. The story spread that either we would be killed that afternoon or some other horrible fate awaited us. At a fast pace, under blows, we were marched through the forest toward the camp three kilometers away.

By the time we got there, many Jews had already been lined up. There was dead silence. The only sounds to be heard were the steps of the returning work groups and the cries of the crows flying overhead. Finally, the camp was called to attention. Feix, with an entourage, including *Unterscharfuehrer* Vetter and *Feldwebel der Schutzpolizei* Adolf Axmann, appeared and said that something terrible had happened and that we would be witnesses to the consequences of the crime committed. From behind us, we heard moans. Somebody was being brought into the camp. A group of Ukrainians led by Polakov, a Ukrainian guard, dragged in a human being, pulling him with barbed wire that had been tied around his neck. He was already quite bloody but was still standing on his own feet. His name was Bitter. He had come in an earlier transport from Warsaw. He was about forty years old.

Earlier, this poor soul had been discovered in the industrial area boiling some potatoes in his tin can. Because a Jew was not supposed to have any potatoes, much less boil them, the guard who found him kicked the can off the fire. The can felt heavier than expected. He examined it, and found a false bottom in which some gold coins were hidden.

Feix called for a scale and for a "mathematician" to weigh the potatoes. He ordered him to multiply the weight by the number of prisoners in the camp. The reasoning was as follows: because each prisoner was responsible for the acts of all the others, all the prisoners were guilty of stealing potatoes. Such acts harmed the heroic German people who were fighting for a just world from which we would all profit. The magnitude of the injury equaled the weight of the potatoes stolen multiplied by the number of prisoners in the camp. Feix therefore decided that, because all the prisoners were guilty, all of us would mete out the punishment: we would beat Bitter to death.

We were standing in the usual formation, long rows around the rectangular *Appellplatz*, five deep. Before we had a chance to comprehend what was happening, the Ukrainians surrounding us began pushing groups of prisoners, five at a time, toward Bitter who was being dragged by the Ukrainian guards. I was the fourth in my line of five. The three men ahead of me moved forward, with other prisoners from other groups. Some of them began to hit Bitter, some with their fists, others with elbows and knees. I backed away. I did not touch him. My conscience did not allow it. I cannot say that I thought the matter through. There was too much panic in the atmosphere. I simply responded by instinct. Some prisoners beat him, figuring that it was an act of mercy to kill him as quickly as possible since his fate was already sealed. Others, including me, could not bring themselves even to touch him. As we moved backwards, trying to get out of the way, the Ukrainians pushing us began clubbing us with their rifle butts, beating us indiscriminately. There was chaos. People were shouting, crying, shoving. Suddenly, shots rang out over our heads. Everything stopped.

Bitter was bleeding from all over, but he was still alive. The Ukrainians, led by the sadists Polakov, Popov, and one whose first name was Otto (Germanized from its original Ukrainian; I never knew his last name) decided that Bitter's condition was not bad enough. They bent his head down and began to burn his eyes with cigarette lighters and matches. While all this was happening, for as long as he was conscious, Bitter cried out as loudly as he could: "*Ich zol zayn a kapore far dem gantsen Klal Yisroel.*" (May I be an atonement for the whole people of Israel.) "*Gott, nem tsi mayn neshome.*" (God, take my soul.) "*Shma Yisroel.*" (Hear, Oh Israel.) At the end, when he was already close to death, they forced a sharpened wooden stake down his throat and poured water into his mouth. When the body did not move any longer, Dr. Mosbach, the Jewish camp physician, was summoned. He declared the man dead.

The body was laid on a stretcher and carried out of the camp to be buried in the forest. Feix ordered that prayers be said and picked several Jews to be "the rabbi" and "the cantor"

Torture and killing of Bitter
Budzyń, 1943

and to recite Psalms. The rest of us were ordered to sing the horrible Marianna tango as the body was taken away. The entire episode, from the time Bitter was brought into the camp until his death, lasted about one and a half hours.

Feix made another speech, insisting that all this was the fault of this one Jew, this pig, who had violated the rules. The same would happen to all others who felt free to do the same. He hoped the rest of our evening would be more pleasant, and invited us to go, eat our dinner, and fill our bellies. We proceeded to our dinner in total silence. By this time, the miserable liquid we received every night was no longer warm. We then went to our barracks. Eventually, we fell asleep.

I do not condemn the people who beat Bitter. They did not act freely. We lived in constant fear of death. Some prisoners were motivated by the desire to end Bitter's suffering. In fact, some were even angry with those who had shied away from beating him. He was doomed anyway, and maybe we could have at least helped him to a speedier, less agonizing death. Nevertheless, every time a Jew died, many of us felt guilty.

Almost all the days in Budzyń were bitter, but some of them were worse than others. Each day, each minute, had the potential for unexpected disasters. Another one of these occurred in the autumn of 1943. Returning to the camp from the work site, we had the feeling that somebody was missing but we were not sure. When the Germans started counting during the lineup, it turned out that one person, a young Jew from Warsaw, was indeed missing. Unfortunately, he belonged to my group of ten. This meant that the other nine of us were dead.

The counting and recounting went on for a long time. The whole camp was kept standing while the count was going on. Crying and wailing broke out among our group of nine when we noticed that we had been surrounded by Ukrainians. They began pushing us toward the main gate. This meant that we were being taken either for interrogation or to the forest to be executed. As we approached the forest, we were ordered to take off our jackets. We felt shots above our heads but no one was hit. Suddenly we saw Stockman, the Jewish head of the prisoners, running toward us accompanied by an SS man. Stockman called me and two other persons out of the line, and the three of us were marched back to the camp.

A corpse lay in the middle of the *Appellplatz*. This was the man who had escaped. He had been captured and killed in the forest, and his body returned to camp for display. Because the escapee had been caught, Stockman had run to Feix's assistant, SS Sergeant Adolf Axmann, to try to persuade him to spare the other nine of us, saying that we were all essential workers, including the *Kunstmahler*. (At the time, I had been working on a piece of art and calligraphy for Axmann). Axmann agreed to spare three of the nine; the saddlemaker, the tailor, both of whom worked for Feix, and me. The other six were executed.

As usual, Feix delivered a speech to the effect that what had happened was our fault. Had we conducted ourselves properly, none of this would have happened. When rules were violated and people tried to escape, they and those who helped them had to pay. In order to emphasize his point, he ordered that the body be hung from the gallows and left there for hours to be viewed by all.

Another horrible day in Budzyń was the one on which Rudi Bauchwitz was hanged. Bauchwitz had been a lieutenant in the German Army in World War I. A tall, handsome man in his fifties, he was popular with the Germans despite his being a Jew, because they saw him also as a German. He

163

worked for them in various capacities in the administration of the camp. To the Polish Jews in the camp, German Jews were objects of respect and interest. Respect, because many were very honorable and had been exposed to Western culture. Interest, because we thought that through them we could learn how the German mind works.

One morning, before going to work, the rumor spread that the gallows were being prepared. We were lined up and Bauchwitz was marched in by Adolf Axmann and Vetter, the two SS officers. They made him mount the platform and told him that he could speak his last words. His last words were that he was going to his death innocent. He concluded by saying: "Death to Hitler and long live a free Germany." He was hanged and his body left on the gallows for the rest of the day.

I do not know what he was accused of. I think he was simply too much for them. They could not deny that he was a German, a former lieutenant in their army, but they could not square this with his being a Jew. He threatened their stereotype of the Jew. He therefore had to die.

As soon as the hanging was over and we had all viewed the body, I was called aside by *Unterscharfuehrer* Vetter and ordered to follow him to his quarters. He took me outside the barbed wire to his living quarters. As he sat down, he made a gesture of disgust, and muttered, "*Scheisse!*" (Shit!) Then he continued, "*Die Sonne ist so schoen, Ich muss in Schatten stehen.*" (The sunshine is so beautiful, and I must stay in the shadow.) I understood what he meant, that there are so many more beautiful things in life than doing this shitty work of hanging prisoners. "*Aber wir müssen das machen!*" he suddenly burst out, "But we have to do it!" He assured me that this morning's hanging had nothing to do with me because that Jew had brought his fate upon himself. I, on the other hand, was a useful Jew who, he prophesied, would survive the war. I just

The hanging of Bauchwitz
Budzyń, 1943

kept standing there, obedient, listening, not knowing what was coming next.

He ordered me to sit down. He pulled out some paper, and told me that I could be helpful to him in connection with his wife's forthcoming birthday. She was in Germany and he wanted to send her a beautifully designed card containing a romantic text. On the left side of the card, I was to draw a Hansel and Gretel house, surrounded by beds of flowers, and on the right side, I was to draw a primitive Polish village full of pigs. Across the bottom, I was to letter in the same text he had recited earlier. This would show the contrast between the sunshine, the beautiful homeland for which he was yearning, and filthy Poland, the shadow in which he found himself at present. It took me about an hour and a half to complete this assignment. He sat and watched me the whole time, drinking vodka mixed with cherry syrup. When I finished the card, he said it was excellent.

He asked me what I had eaten for breakfast. I jumped to my feet, snapped to attention and replied that I had had some ersatz *kaffee*, warm water with chicory, as per regulations. He snapped at me, "*Scheisse!*" (Shit!) He ordered one of the Jewish female prisoners who worked in the SS quarters, Hannelore, to serve me a full officers' breakfast consisting of toast, scrambled eggs fried in butter, and real coffee with milk and sugar. He watched me as I ate, drinking whiskey. I ate, and thought my stomach would burst, I was so uncomfortable with him staring at me throughout. He asked me when was the last time I had eaten such a breakfast. I told him that I could not remember. Then he walked me back to camp, about five minutes away.

When we entered the camp, he took me to Stockman, and, to my utter amazement and horror, started screaming at him, shoving his whip under his nose: how dare he send the *Kunstmahler* to Vetter's quarters wearing clothing as dirty as mine and smelling as bad as I did! Stockman stood as still as a statue, apologized profusely, and said that I would immediately be supplied with clean clothing. Vetter replied that this should have been done before I was sent to him and not after. He would overlook it this time, but if it happened again, Stockman would pay for it.

I was horrified because it sounded as if I had complained to Vetter about Stockman. When Stockman took me to the clothing barrack, he asked me what had happened. I explained that Vetter had made me draw a card for him and had served me a decent breakfast, but that he had said nothing about my clothing until we returned to the camp. I was afraid that this would affect our relationship, but Noah cut me off, telling me that he didn't need any explanation further, that he knew me and trusted me.

The man in charge of the clothing storehouse handed me a woolen navy blue jacket with a spot of blood on it. I got scared when I saw it. Not because of the blood, which I was used to, but because the jacket had belonged to the head of the Jewish community of Kraśnik, Pesach Kava, whom everyone had known and respected. Kava had been tortured to death by Feix for not turning over gold supposedly hidden by the Kraśnik Jewish community. Now I was given his jacket to wear, with a shirt and a pair of pants taken from the piles of clothing stripped from the dead. I scrubbed off the bloodstain with a little water, and wore this clothing until a few months later, when I was given striped prison pajamas.

In this chapter, I have described some particularly painful episodes that are inscribed in my memory. But those days, terrible as they were, were not much worse than so-called normal days. Death was with us every day. People were badly beaten every day. Prisoners died of illness and starvation every day. So while there were days that were particularly bad, the rest were not much better.

17

In the autumn of 1943, the Jewish leadership of the camp—Jewish POWs from the Polish army and some Kapos—started planning an escape. They even began digging a tunnel. It started in one of the barracks and was supposed to extend under the barbed wire fence, surfacing in a nearby field. The earth that was removed in the process of digging had to be carried out each morning in the clothing of the people involved, and dumped on the way to work. This was not easy because we were constantly being guarded, but apparently a good piece of the tunnel had been dug when the plan was abandoned.

I did not learn of this plan while it was underway. Only after it was abandoned did Noah Stockman tell me about it. From the beginning, he and some others, including several rabbis, were against it. They felt that it was suicidal. Feix would take extreme measures against those remaining in the camp. Even if we got out of the camp, we could not survive outside for very long. The Germans were constantly fighting partisan units in the surrounding Lublin forests and would certainly catch most of the escaped Jews. We had no weapons and the peasants in the surrounding villages lived in fear of German reprisals. In addition, many were not very friendly to Jews.

It was not easy to convince those who favored this plan to abandon it. The argument that finally worked was the belief that, because Budzyń was a labor camp, and we were productive workers, our chances of survival seemed better than average.

On November 4, 1943, a number of healthy prisoners were loaded onto trucks and driven away. In the evening, they returned in trucks full of clothing, some of which was soaked in blood. They had been taken to Majdanek, the mother camp of Budzyń, forty-eight kilometers away. While they had been loading the clothing, they were told by Polish prisoners that the day before, November 3, 1943, all 18,500 Jews in Majdanek had been executed by the Germans to the sound of German music. (I found out later that my dear friend, Izak Rubin the lithographer, who had helped keep me alive during those difficult months in the ghetto, had been among those murdered.) That same day, all the Jews in Trawniki and Poniatowa (subcamps of Majdanek) were also murdered.

The news that the Jews of the surrounding camps had been murdered depressed us profoundly. Yet, the fact that their clothing had been transferred to us gave us hope. It confirmed our belief that we were being prepared to survive the winter.

All that fall, the German leadership of the camp changed hands. Feix left, and was replaced by Adolf Axmann, followed by Mohr, Schragner, Vetter, and finally Tauscher.

Sometimes we were not even sure who the commandant was. All of them ordered and participated in killings and torture.

At one evening *Appell,* a father and his four sons were brought before the commandant, Mohr. One son had been accused of stealing potatoes. Mohr asked the father to verify that this was his son. The father did. Mohr said, "He stole potatoes. I want you to hang him." The father refused. Mohr said, "Then I'm going to make him hang you!" The son answered, "No. You can kill me but I'm not going to hang my father." Mohr said, "Then all five of you will be killed."

We were standing in the usual rectangular formation, around the *Appellplatz.* We were ordered to open the rectangle to form a U-shape, so there was open space at one end. These five people were made to stand in front of that open area, facing away from the camp, with the father in the middle and two sons on each side. Mohr ordered five Ukrainian guards, who stood behind the five victims to shoot them in the back of the head. The flashes from their rifles blazed against the darkness of the sky.

During another evening lineup in November, SS *Untersturmfuehrer* Tauscher, the new commandant, announced that the camp was in danger of being attacked by Polish partisans. For our own good, "to protect us," the doors to the barracks would be barred from now on by heavy beams secured from the outside. We would therefore be unable to leave the barracks until the beams were removed in the morning.

Shortly before dawn, we heard trucks and soldiers moving around the camp. Each barrack was surrounded by the SS and Ukrainians armed with machine guns. But nothing happened. At 7:00 A.M. the barrack gates were opened and we proceeded with our usual activities. We understood later that we had been marked for death, that the Germans routinely barricaded barracks in this way whenever they planned to murder an entire camp. While the inhabitants of one barrack were being killed, those in the other barracks could not escape because they were locked in. The units surrounding us during the night had been *Einsatzgruppen,* special killing squads, ready for action. At the last moment, the plan to murder everyone in the camp had been cancelled. The German civilian leadership of the industrial plants where we worked (including Karl Jaeger, Stepan, Hentze, the architect in charge of the construction unit, and others), together with the SS camp leadership, had appealed to the High Command in Berlin to spare us because we were useful laborers.

They did this to save their own skins. They ran a magnificent operation: killing Jews, collecting gold, living in comfortable surroundings with their families, and impressing the Command in Berlin that their work was essential to the war effort. This kept them safe, far from the Russian front to which they probably would have been sent had Berlin decided to close these operations down.

Our camp was the only one in the entire district of Lublin that was saved from death.

One night in January, 1944, I was awakened by screams and the sound of shooting. At this time, I was no longer sleeping in my former barrack, Barrack 5. Because I was often summoned to work closely with the Germans and they were very much afraid of epidemics carried by lice, they felt safer if I was not in close contact with the other prisoners. They transferred me to Barrack 6, which contained a small cubicle set off from the main barrack. This cubicle contained three sleeping shelves. I slept on one, and a Warsaw lawyer named Lewitan and his son slept on the other two.

The shooting outside the barracks that night was so intense that the sky lit up as if it were day. Suddenly the door to our cubicle was ripped open and several Ukrainian guards appeared. The first one who crashed in, his rifle pointed at us, was Michaiło. Several weeks earlier, I had designed a Christmas card for him that he planned to send home to his mother. When he recognized me, he ordered the three of us to drop to the floor. He told us to keep still and not to worry. He slammed the door shut and left with the others.

In the morning we learned that, earlier that night, a few prisoners had tried to escape through the latrine, the building nearest the barbed-wire fence. A guard in the watchtower had spotted them and sounded the alarm. In addition to those who had made the attempt, about fifty Jews were dragged out from their barracks and murdered that night. My having done a drawing for Michailo had saved the lives of the three of us in the cubicle.

In the morning, the lineup was delayed and finally conducted on the blood-drenched, snow-covered field in sub-zero temperature. We were forced to stand motionless for several hours as punishment for the attempted escape. *Kommandant* Tauscher delivered a long speech. We did not appreciate what the camp authorities were doing for us, he said. Here they were protecting us from the dangers that lurked in the surrounding vicinity by keeping us safe in the camp. And this is how we showed our gratitude—by attempting to escape. Finally, the corpses were taken off to be buried, fresh snow covered the bloody field and the camp went back to its normal routine.

Shortly after this incident, rumors began circulating that the camp would be moved to a different location. At first we were skeptical, but we soon found out that a new camp was indeed being erected several kilometers away. We also observed that some of our barracks were being dismantled.

One day, toward the end of January, we were kept in the

camp and not allowed to go to work. We heard screams coming from various barracks, especially the women's. Groups of prisoners were loaded onto trucks. Some were naked, others half-naked. It was obvious that we would never see them again, although we did not know exactly where they were being taken. When this was finished, the rest of us were sent to our usual work. The next day, the move began, and the entire camp was transferred over the course of several days. I never found out the reason for the move.

The new camp was somewhat larger than the old one. I felt much more imprisoned there because its barbed-wire fence was electrified, making it even more escape-proof. In addition, a new SS leadership took over, and any change was frightening. The new commandant was *Untersturmfuehrer* Leipold, a man in his mid-thirties, blond, with a military bearing. He somehow seemed less threatening, less dangerous, than the commandants who had gone before him. I later learned that he loved art. At his first appearance, Leipold delivered the usual speech about hard work and the good results that would follow from strict obedience to the rules.

This new camp was considered a concentration camp, while the former one had been a labor camp. A concentration camp was run with more discipline. All infractions, such as carrying a metal spoon, a potential weapon, were punished by death. While the same punishment might have been meted out in the old camp, there it was often the result of the commandant's personal sadism (as with Feix), while here it was required by the regulations. For the first time, we received striped clothing and a number, stenciled in black onto a small rectangular piece of white fabric next to a red and yellow six-pointed Star of David. We had to attach it onto our clothing ourselves; prisoners working in the camp tailor shops did this for us with a few stitches in each corner. My number, which I wore over my heart as per regulations, was 448.

Our sleeping facilities were about the same as before but the food improved a little. The soup contained a little more edible content: a few more potatoes or other vegetables, a little barley.

A week or so after our arrival at the new site, a Jew escaped while at work outside the camp. He was caught toward evening and brought back to the camp. He was made to drop his pants and kneel over a stool while he was given twenty-five lashes. After this, bleeding badly, he was forced to stand between the two strands of electrified barbed wire, holding a log on his shoulders. The entire camp had to stand out in the icy cold and watch this agony. About 2:00 A.M. he was removed from between the fences and the camp was dismissed without supper. I do not know what happened to him after we were dismissed.

On the other side of the barbed wire, several barracks had been built. We did not know the purpose of these barracks at first, but after a while we noticed that *Wehrmacht* units were quartered there. Each group only stayed for a few days before moving on, probably rotating to and from the Eastern front. Many of the soldiers seemed to be curious about the prisoners on the other side of the barbed wire. One evening, a prisoner was being beaten in view of the entire camp, as usual. Suddenly, we heard shouting from the other side of the fence. A *Wehrmacht* captain was berating Leipold, calling him a "*Judenheld*" (hero of the Jews). He added: "Why don't you go and be a hero on the Eastern front?" Leipold was, of course, infuriated by these remarks in the presence of the prisoners. He ran to the fence, pulled out his gun and threatened to kill the captain. The captain retreated. We were shocked and pleased to see such friction between Germans, especially such an outburst from a regular army man toward the SS. We also knew that this would not help us in any way.

18

Toward the end of January, 1944, I was ordered to appear before Leipold. He asked me what my artistic specialty was and whether I worked in oils. I replied in the affirmative. He then took me to his quarters, unrolled a number of canvasses and asked if I recognized any of them. Some I did, some I did not. He said that he was particularly interested in a Delacroix landscape. A friend of his had left a real Delacroix with him and he wanted a copy made for himself. I told him that I would do my best but I needed a canvas and paint. He replied that he would get a car and a driver and send me to Lublin to obtain whatever I needed.

I was wearing the striped clothing of a prisoner and my head was shaven. I could not very well appear in this guise in Lublin. He got me a pair of overalls and a cap. With an SS man as both my driver and my guard, I made the hour-long trip to Lublin and went from store to store, finding what I needed. Wherever I went, my SS guard followed me, filling out vouchers for everything we got. These were, of course, worthless. The Poles were not going to argue with an SS man and were only too glad to give him whatever he wanted and get him out of the store as quickly as possible.

Back at camp, Leipold assigned me a place to work in a barrack, which I shared with Jakob Eljowicz, the portrait photographer for the SS. I did not have to do my usual tasks outside the camp but could concentrate on the painting. I divided the original canvas into squares and proceeded to copy each square as accurately as I could. Leipold often came to watch me work. After about three weeks, the job was finished. He was satisfied and gave me a whole pack of cigarettes.

In February, 1944, I was summoned to the SS building. Leipold again ordered me to change out of my striped prisoners' clothing into a pair of overalls and a cap. He took me to his office and told me to select paper and drawing instruments. He walked with me to an automobile and got behind the wheel. He told me to get in, wrap myself in a sheet that was in the car, and sit as far as possible from him so that he would not catch any disease from me. He drove us to the outskirts of Kraśnik, a drive of about forty-five minutes, to a small camp which housed some Jewish artisans. There was a commotion in the camp, with many soldiers milling around, some holding bloodhounds. There had been an escape. Leipold explained to the camp SS authorities that I was an artist and ordered me to draw the plan of the camp, the suspected escape route, and the damaged section of the barbed-wire fence. The drawing was to accompany a written report being sent to SS headquarters. While he had lunch with his SS friends, I completed my assignment. Then he sent me back to the camp in a half-track in which I was guarded by two German shepherds, SS attack dogs.

Sometime after this incident, the rumor spread that Leipold had been wounded. Indeed, he appeared with a cast on his right foot. Later, Dr. Mosbach told us that he suspected that Leipold had shot himself in the foot, presumably in order to escape being sent to the Russian front. Following this incident, Leipold seemed to become less dangerous than he had been before. Our food got a little better and there were no public beatings.

One of my artistic functions in Budzyń was to paint caskets. These were plain pine coffins, which I painted black with a silver cross on the top. On the horizontal bar of the cross, I painted the words *Ruhe Sanft!* (Rest in peace!) in Gothic script, and on the side of the coffin, I painted the name of the deceased, his date of birth and the date of death. One day, a soldier fell under the wheel of a transport wagon and was killed. I prepared his coffin, painted in his name, Pfeiffer, and continued working on some other caskets that were stacked up nearby, drying. The Germans became nervous because they had to load the body to be taken away and they couldn't locate his coffin immediately, as it was piled among the others. SS *Unterscharfuehrer* Schragner picked up a chair and threw it at me, hitting me. Just then, someone else yelled that they had found the casket. They drove it away, presumably to load the body and bury it in a nearby field. Schragner, of course, did not apologize; his "apology" was that he didn't beat me again.

The cross with its "rest in peace" painted on the caskets, the crosses that some Germans wore, the fact that officially we did not work on Sundays and occasionally got slightly better food at Christmas—these were the only signs of anything related to Christianity I ever saw throughout the camps. I did not know whether these gestures reflected true belief or custom or superstition. If I expected to see evidence of religious,

179

ethical behavior, these I did not see. What I saw was beating, shooting, murder. What I heard was *Judas,* a word associated with hatred for the Jews. I had never been able to get out of my mind the text I had been ordered to paint in the canteen at Okęcie airfield, *In der Bibel ist geschrieben, Du sollst auch deine Feinde lieben.* (In the Bible, it is written, you should also love your enemies.) How could they quote the Bible and do what they were doing?

On April 19, 1944, I was among a group of Jews taken to the building that housed the SS. I was chosen because I was the *Kunstmahler.* Our task was to decorate the front of the building in honor of the *Fuehrer*'s birthday the following day, April 20. They brought in a fire truck with a four-story-high ladder, which I had to climb to attach a huge wreath to the front of the building. Inside the wreath, I placed a large picture of the *Fuehrer,* and on both sides of it I hung huge swastika flags. When we were finished, for some reason that I cannot fathom even today, I mentioned to one of the Jews that April 20 also happened to be my birthday. I was a fool to have said it, and in Yiddish. Had I spoken Polish, none of the Germans would have understood what I said. As it happened, however, my remark was overheard by one of the SS guards. He asked me to repeat this statement. I did, and he clubbed me with the butt of his rifle. SS *Unterscharfuehrer* Schragner, supervising nearby, asked me whether what I had said was true or a lie. I said it was true. He replied that it was not possible for a Jew to be born on the same day as the *Fuehrer.* He added that if I could make up a lie like this, I did not deserve to live. He ordered me to stand by the wall, picked up a stool and threw it at me. I ducked. The stool sailed past me into the wall, and one of its legs broke off. He was furious. He screamed at me to stand erect and not move. If I moved, he would shoot me, and to underscore the threat, he unsnapped the holster of his gun. He threw the stool at my head. It hit me in the mouth, and blood poured down. I thought he was going to kill me; usually when they saw blood, they went into a killing frenzy, like sharks. But for some reason he did not finish the job. I was permitted to return to camp and wash my bloody body. I lost a row of teeth. I made a vow never to forget this event of April 20.

In spring 1944, a new transport of Jews arrived in Budzyń. They were from Hrubieszów, in eastern Poland. This indicated to us that the front was moving towards us. Soon after that, we were told that the camp was going to be moved again—further west—further proof that the war was not going well for the Germans. A number of selections took place and no one knew where those selected were sent. Some of these groups—the weakest people in the camp—were clearly marked for death. But other groups seemed to be selected for work. One group consisted of printers, lithographers, and precision mechanics. My good friend, Szyja Hochrad, the master watch repairman, was among them. I did not volunteer for this group. I did not want to take any risks, because people involved with graphics were considered dangerous, potentially linked to anti-Nazi activities. I did not want to gamble with my fate. After the war, I learned that they were sent to Oranienburg and put to work on counterfeiting projects.

About May, we were all loaded into freight trains and shipped to various camps. Mayer Lachman was shipped to Radom, and from there to Auschwitz. Others were sent to Gross-Rosen, or to Oranienburg. The trains were smaller this time—three, four, five cars each. The doors of the car I was in were not closed but a guard with a gun sat just inside each door. Straw had been laid in the cars and approximately forty-five persons were put in each one, a number that made the trip quite comfortable. We were also given a loaf of bread and a can of cheese, and water was provided. This was extraordinary and we could not understand the reason for the generosity.

After we had traveled several hours, the train stopped, probably to let other trains pass. Leipold permitted us to get off the train and take care of our bodily needs. Meanwhile, he sat on a chair near the train and was given a haircut and a shave by Sommer, a Jewish barber from Lwów. The scene, on a beautiful sunny spring day, was unusually peaceful. I attribute all this to Leipold, whose behavior was unusually decent under the circumstances.

We traveled southwest, in the direction of Cracow. The following day, midmorning, we arrived at Wieliczka, an area of salt mines in southwestern Poland. Wieliczka, a subcamp of Auschwitz, already held about two thousand Jews; our transport increased the number by about nine hundred.

Much of our reception at the camp was the usual one, including delousing and warnings against escape. This was a particularly sensitive subject in this camp because it was located on the outskirts of the Polish town of Wieliczka rather than in a remote area. However, some things were new. The middle of our heads was shaved to mark us as prisoners. This shaven strip was called the *Lausestrasse* (Lice Street). I was given a new number, 22298. But the major difference was that, for the first time, they tattooed us. The letters *KL*, for *Konzentrationslager*, were tattooed onto our left forearms, above the wrist, about where the face of a watch would be. Dr. Mosbach, assisted by a German soldier, did the tattooing using a four-pronged instrument dipped in ink with which he pierced the skin, thereby injecting the ink under the skin. This caused bleeding and swelling and took several days to heal.

I was not reconciled to accepting this tattoo. My reaction was simple and instinctive: I did not want this mark on me. I also had never stopped thinking about escape, and a tattoo would make it almost impossible to disguise myself should I ever get out. Throughout the night, I sucked at my arm, sucking out the ink. By morning, the tattoo was gone. Several days later, during a lineup, they ordered us to show our forearms so they could check the tattoo. Had they found my wrist without it, I would have been in serious trouble because this would be proof of my desire to escape. Fortunately, I had a pencil on me and quickly wrote *KL* on my wrist. This fooled them.

The next day we were taken to the salt mines, about two kilometers away from the entrance to the camp. We were assigned to the Heinkel repair works, which were located in the mines.

We were taken by elevator into shafts several hundred feet deep in a mysterious world of underground lakes and passages, all of salt. The salt mines themselves were still very much in operation. Gentile Poles, paid miners with labor ID cards, lived in the town with their families and worked in the mines, chopping away the salt by hand, loading it onto little cars on tracks, and transporting it to the surface. Occasionally, they shared information about the progress of the war with us.

Being in the salt mines was scary at first, because I did not know what the Germans had in mind for us, and because it was such a mysterious new world—phenomenal, but treacherous. You walked between huge open flat areas and tremendous lakes. One push, and you could fall into an abyss of several hundred feet, or into the lakes. The work areas were set up in huge level areas the size of dance halls. Electric lights were strung overhead, under enormous vaulting "ceilings" from which salt water dripped continuously. It was cold and wet and quite uncomfortable for us with our thin clothing and starved bodies.

I was put to work repairing damaged Heinkel airplane parts, mostly wings, with a hydraulic riveting gun. The entire operation struck me as inefficient. Everything seemed to move in slow motion. People, exhausted to death, were required to do jobs they were unqualified for. I wondered whether this factory was another fake, whose real purpose was to keep the commanders safe, far away from the front. I worked there for about six weeks.

The camp was right at the edge of the town of Wieliczka. We lived in small, dilapidated houses, surrounded by wire fences with an open field beyond them. From the windows of my room on the second floor of one of these houses, I could see Poles walking about freely on the street. I thought—as always—about escape. Until I realized that I couldn't escape. I could be caught by a German, I could be caught by a Pole, I had no place to go, I had no money, my head was shaven and it would take at least a month before the hair grew in fully.

One day, SS *Kommandant* Schragner decided to keep his horse at an old stable located on the estate that housed the SS, just outside the barbed-wire fence of the camp. He had the structure renovated and now wanted it painted. He chose me for the job and told me to select whatever help I needed. I picked the three men closest to me and we started working. Schragner gave us only one and a half hours to complete the job, because this was a private job and he was not supposed to be taking us away from our work in the salt mines. The penalty for not completing the job on time was death. We worked at such a frantic pace that I fell off a ladder and knocked over a bucket of whitewash. It fell on my right foot, injuring the big toe. When he came back at the end of the hour and a half, the job was done to his satisfaction.

My toe became infected and I suffered for weeks. I even developed a high fever that lasted several days. My friend, Yehuda Gram, took care of me, applying cold compresses of my urine—we had no water—to my toe and head whenever he could. I worked steadily throughout this period despite the injury. After a while, it cleared up.

It was in this camp that I made the acquaintance of two brothers who were destined to become particularly close friends of mine. It was mid-morning on a rainy day. I was working in an empty barrack, drawing a large portrait of Schragner's girlfriend from a photograph he had given me. As I worked, I noticed a group of Jews outside, digging a ditch. I opened the window to look at the poor souls digging in the rain, and two of the men moved toward me. They looked inside the barrack and saw the photograph pinned to a board and the sheet of paper on which I was drawing. This surprised them and our eyes met. Somehow, this established an immediate relationship. I invited them inside and we began to talk. They were the brothers Simon and Alexander (Sandor) Sagh, in their late forties and early fifties. They came from Beregszasz in Hungary. Simon was a physician and Alexander, a dentist. They had been brought to Wieliczka from Auschwitz, where their wives had been selected for the gas chambers.

After this, we were inseparable. I was present later at their deaths but this was still in the future.

19

We heard reports from Poles with whom some Jews were in contact that the Allies were approaching and the Russian front was getting closer. Clearly, the war was going against the Germans. We noticed a steady deterioration in the psychological condition of the SS. Some became more disorganized, more nervous. Some became more meek, others more vicious.

Early in September 1944, we were packed into railroad cars and taken to our new camp, Płaszów, near Cracow. This was a huge concentration camp, a subcamp of Auschwitz. For the first time, we were supervised by non-Jewish German prisoners. They wore a green down-pointed triangle with the letters *BV* inscribed in it, for *Berufsverbrecher* (Professional Criminal). After serving part of their sentences in prison, they were transferred to concentration camps to assist the SS. By doing so, they were contributing to the war effort of the

Fatherland. Their status was somewhere between that of prisoner and guard, probably closer to guard.

Płaszów was a very well-organized camp that had already been in operation for several years. There were various shops utilizing the skills of a variety of trades: tailors, mechanics, shoemakers, and the like. Outside the camp, large work forces were kept busy digging ditches, for defense, for burial. The well-known Jewish musicians, the Rosner brothers, directed the camp orchestra; the commandant, when I arrived, was Amon Goeth, murderer and music lover.

We arrived in Płaszów shortly before Rosh Hashanah. We were not well received by the Jews already there. The Jewish camp leadership had recently suffered a severe blow to their morale. Several weeks earlier, the Jewish head of the camp, Chilewicz, had been accused of bribing some Ukrainians to help him escape in a truck. The Ukrainians took his gold and then turned him over to the Germans. He and his wife and family were brought back to camp, tortured, and executed. This had a devastating effect on morale because the Jews had thought that, in this camp, their chances of surviving were quite good. The murder of Chilewicz, who had supposedly had a good relationship with the Germans, severely shook whatever confidence they had had. Then we showed up. The arrival of new prisoners with their own leadership always constituted a threat to the establishment, but coming on the heels of the death of their own leadership, this was a double threat.

For the first few days we were in Płaszów, we were engaged in useless labor, digging ditches, lugging rocks from one place to another and back again. Maybe they just did not know what to do with us. Then, about a week after my arrival, around six o'clock in the evening, the SS lined up about one hundred of us, taking down our names and numbers. This was a strange and alarming procedure, which I had never experienced before. Whatever activity they had in store for us, they wanted to know precisely which of us were involved in it, to be able to track us down later. They gave each of us a shovel or a pick and marched us out of the camp and up a hill, a march of about half an hour. We began to smell a terrible odor. We had arrived at our destination.

We were at a place called Hujowa Góra, where ten thousand Jews had been killed. In front of us were huge open pits containing the remains of corpses. We were ordered to exhume the bodies.

The ditches were about twenty feet deep, and you climbed in and out of them on primitive ladders made of logs lashed together. At the bottom of the ditches, the diggers (*Ausgrabungskommando*) were at work. Using shovels and picks, they located the bodies and dug them out of the earth. Once the bodies had been freed, the diggers placed them on wooden stretchers for the carriers who dragged the bodies up the ladders and out of the pit. Another group of workers, the burners (*Verbrennungskommando*), would stack the bodies between layers of logs for burning at dawn. The burning was not done at night so as not to attract the attention of Allied planes.

I was working with several Jews, including the Grosman family from Kraśnik, a father and his two sons, and Itzhak Dorfsman, whose assistance in some of my artwork had spared him from a deadly "selection." We decided to leave as many bodies as possible in the earth for religious reasons. Judaism insists on quick burial of the dead and does not generally permit disinterment. We felt that disturbing the rest of the dead was a desecration and it was our duty to keep this desecration to a minimum. At one point, we found the body of a mother clutching a child against her breast. This shattered us even more than the rest and we decided to hide these two bodies at any cost. So while we kept uncovering other bodies, we covered these bodies with earth. As we did so, one of us recited the *Kaddish*.

Some of the bodies had been buried almost a year, while others had been murdered more recently. Bodies that are several months old come apart easily when lifted. You lifted a body, and the skin would slide off the bones like a glove, leaving you with just the skin in your hands. We collected pieces of bodies, heads, hands, legs, intestines, all of which were falling apart.

We were working at night by the illumination of floodlights that had been set up at the edges of the pits. After a while, we became oblivious to the smell. The work was done at a very fast tempo, hurried on by screams and beatings with axes and picks. The horror of the scene cannot be described.

The scene was too much for the SS. They stayed back at a distance and got drunk. The actual supervision was done by German Kapos and Ukrainian guards. Directly in charge was a German BV (Professional Criminal) Kapo nicknamed Ivan by the prisoners. (We never knew his real name, and I don't know exactly why he got this nickname. Maybe his cruelty reminded someone of the historic Ivan the Terrible.) His specialty, I observed, was to kill by means of a kick to the groin. When the person fell to the ground, he would step on his throat, killing him.

About midnight, after we had worked about six hours, the floodlights suddenly went out and we were driven to a particular spot on a hill. We heard sirens sounding in the distance and knew that it was an air attack. But we saw no planes. They ordered us to wash our hands in a disinfectant and rinse them with water. After that, dinner was served. We received a thicker soup and a half a loaf of bread each, far more than our usual diet.

As we were eating, the word spread: "Jews, tonight is Rosh Hashanah." There were deep sighs, but not much more of a reaction. We were actually no longer alive.

When we finished our dinner, we were marched to another nearby hill where several large German military trucks were lined up with their backs toward the pits. In the trucks were the naked bodies of men and women, very recently killed. Some of the mouths were sealed with plaster. We were told that this was done to prevent the person from screaming while allowing him to still breathe through the nose. It never became clear to me why it was necessary to prevent people from screaming. We were told that these Jews had been captured in hiding, or posing as Aryans with false papers. They were tortured and killed in a Cracow prison, and transported to Płaszów to be burned. On other occasions, they were brought alive—with their mouths sealed—to Płaszów, where they were executed, and then burned.

Our detail went to work emptying the trucks. Some bodies were carried by four persons, most were dragged by two. Because these were recently killed bodies, they did not come apart as did bodies that had been buried for some time. We had to work very fast though, carrying each body several hundred feet from the trucks to the pyres that would be lit at dawn. This work exhausted us physically and emotionally because of the terror, the beatings, and the screams that accompanied everything. The Germans' favorite screams were "tempo," "let's go," and "make it fast, you dirty pigs."

By the third trip, I could not take it any longer. I lay down next to a mound of dead bodies so that I would blend in with them. But Ivan spotted me from the top of the pit, jumped down like a wild beast and struck me on my left elbow with his pick. Luckily, the blow struck me broadside and I took off like a wounded animal toward the running Jews. I continued working the rest of the night. My arm hurt badly and after a while it swelled up. But I could pay no attention to it. I had to work.

Toward dawn, as we were finishing our work, the pyres were soaked with gasoline and lit. They exploded and the bodies began moving around in a ghostly dance of death. The movement was caused by the force of the explosions and the heat bursting the bodies. This hellish scene of bodies and flames against the still-dark sky is something I will never forget.

In the morning we were again made to wash our hands in disinfectant liquid. Upon our return to the camp, we were isolated in special barracks and allowed to sleep until about two in the afternoon. Because my arm had swelled up as a result of Ivan's blow, I went to the first-aid station for medical attention. Dr. Gross from Cracow asked me what had happened. I was afraid to tell him the truth. There was an unwritten code that you never complained about anything, especially not the actions of the Germans or their henchmen. In addition, I was afraid to disclose what I had been doing when the injury occurred, or where I had been working, because it was obviously a secret operation. I simply told him that I fell. He would not excuse me from work; in his view, my injury was not that serious. Yehuda Gram again applied urine compresses to my injured arm. It was the only remedy we had. By five o'clock, we had to line up again to receive the shovels and picks and then we were marched back to continue digging up the dead.

I worked at this place for about a week. As time went by, instead of becoming easier, it became more difficult. I felt I was losing my mind, that I would not survive if this continued. On the fifth day, I decided to talk to somebody in authority to get another work assignment. The chief Kapo was a German criminal prisoner by the name of Erich, a powerfully built, heavy-set man with a reputation for being easy-going. After waking up in the afternoon, I washed myself as well as I could to get rid of the horrible odor of death that clung to me and went to see him. I told him that the work I had been doing for almost a week was unbearable to me. I would be more productive doing something that utilized my skill as an artist. He told me to be patient, to continue my work for a few more days, and he would see what he could do. About three days later, the Jewish foreman of the death brigade told me that I would be reassigned the following day. I began to work in a barrack involved in various activities, such as drafting and sign painting. I also prepared some sort of dials, drawing wavelength numbers and the names of cities on pieces of glass that were cut to fit some kind of equipment, maybe radios. I don't know what they did with these dials but, in any case, it was better than digging up the dead. I was also moved into a regular barrack and was given a new set of clothing because the smell from my old clothing was unbearable. I sought out Erich to thank him. He smiled and seemed to feel good about it.

20

I was in Płaszów about six weeks. One morning, toward the end of October, 1944, I was again loaded onto a train in an all-male transport and moved west. With me were my dear friends, Alexander and Simon Sagh. The trip lasted almost twenty-four hours, stop and go, and the next day we arrived at the concentration camp Flossenbürg, in Bavaria. We stayed there overnight. The next day we were again selected and loaded onto a train. We traveled for another day until we arrived at our destination, the concentration camp in Zschachwitz near Dresden. This camp was in a huge complex of factory buildings that had been the *Miag Werke* producing milling machines before the war. It had been converted into a tank-building factory. There were about fifteen hundred prisoners in Zschachwitz. Most of these were not Jews but Ukrainians, Italians, Greeks, a few British, Russians, and German political and criminal prisoners. There was also a big contingent of Poles, brought from Warsaw following the general uprising there in August, 1944.

We were received in a vast hall. Suspended above us were tracks with massive hooks and winches capable of lifting the bodies of tanks and transporting them around the factory. The reception here was better than at a regular concentration camp with its smell of death, the terrifying discipline, the screaming, the beatings. *Feldwebel* Marx, the camp commandant, gave the usual speech, telling us that we were in a factory in Germany, that we would have to comply with orders, and that violating any rule would be considered sabotage and have grave consequences. However, his attitude and behavior were rather those of a professional boss giving an orientation to his workers.

Marx was particularly interested in finding out which prisoners had technological skills. Simon and Alexander Sagh reported that they were doctors and were assigned to the camp infirmary. I stepped forward and reported that I was a graphic artist. Nevertheless, the next morning I was put to work in the factory, in the *Sorterei*, sorting metal parts, cleaning, polishing, and taking inventory. Some technically qualified prisoners were put to work on lathes and other heavy machinery. A few days later, I was assigned to the *Harterei:* entire bodies of Tiger 52 tanks were heated to a particular temperature and then quickly dropped into a huge vat containing a chemical bath which hardened the steel. The chemicals gave off poisonous vapors that caused coughing and respiratory damage. Only the German workers were given protective masks.

For the most part, however, the biggest danger we faced was starvation combined with the extremely heavy physical labor. Our diet consisted of warm chicory liquid in the morning and some thin soup at noon. In the evening, we got about three slices of bread made of flour and sawdust, a tablespoon of marmalade or margarine, and a little more thin soup or chicory liquid. Over time, such a diet will kill anyone, particularly when one is doing hard physical labor. There was such hunger in the camp that a group of Ukrainians ran a little business for themselves, slicing off pieces of flesh from some of the dead bodies in the morgue, broiling them and selling them to starving prisoners. When word of this reached the authorities, they caught the Ukrainians and had them beaten severely.

Our supervisors were German civilians, not prisoners. We worked from ten to twelve hours a day, six days a week. On Sunday, everything stopped and we had a day off, though we had to clean our quarters. The atmosphere was not one of terror, though there was very strict discipline. The one thing that resulted in terrible beatings was actual or suspected sabotage. Slowing down the assembly line by an individual or a group was considered sabotage.

About a month after my arrival in Zschachwitz, I was summoned to Marx's quarters. He must have remembered my reporting that I was an artist when we first arrived. He asked me whether I could work in pastels. When I said that I could, he handed me a large box of pastels. He offered me real coffee and a slice of good bread and then ordered me to make a color enlargement of a black-and-white photograph of his wife and three children, in pastels. He told me that he had once studied art in the Academy of Fine Arts in Dresden.

At first, I continued working in the tank plant while doing this assignment part time. Then Marx transferred me to the medical station attached to the plant, at the suggestion of my dear friends, Simon and Alexander Sagh, who ran this station. The medical staff included an Italian physician from Turin, an ardent Communist, by the name of Aliberti. There was also Dr. Josef Mandel, an Austrian gentile dentist from Gratz, who was a political prisoner.

I worked as a male nurse, feeding and cleaning the patients, most of whom had typhus and severe diarrhea. Later, I was able to get Kurt Buchenholz assigned to the infirmary as a male nurse as well. His health had been deteriorating. As hospital workers, we got a little more food than regular prisoners—half a bread daily, instead of the usual three slices—and this helped him recuperate.

Because most of the patients who entered this medical station died, a morgue was set up next door under the supervision of a young Polish Jew by the name of Krebs.

Although Alexander was a dentist, he was made an assistant to his brother Simon and did the work of a physician. Simon, a few years older, was the more serious of the two. Alexander had an easier outlook on life and a great sense of humor. He had enjoyed traveling and had visited almost every city in Europe. He could talk endlessly about the museums and concert halls and other attractions in each.

Both Sagh brothers developed a good relationship with the Germans, including the SS leadership, the administration of the factory, the district doctor, and the German Kapos. They were both respected, particularly Simon who saved many lives. When one of the German Kapos beat a prisoner, Simon would intervene, inviting him in for a talk. He would talk mildly, first agreeing with the Kapo that, of course, he was absolutely right, the prisoner did break the rules, and then gradually appealing to his sympathy. On a number of occasions, he was able to calm the Kapo down and save the prisoner.

One night, Simon disappeared, only to reappear the next morning, looking pale and worn out. Later he told me, in the strictest confidence, that he had performed a service for the SS Commandant. Ironically, this was Tauscher, who had previously been in Budzyń and reappeared now in Zschachwitz. Tauscher had driven Simon to a hospital to perform an abortion. The woman, who was the wife of a civilian factory administrator, had become pregnant by the SS commandant. Tauscher appeared to be grateful to Simon. We received additional medical supplies, including aspirin and Prontosil, a red pill that was supposed to be useful in fighting infections.

A military medical team from Dresden injected the prisoners with an inoculation against typhus. We did not know if these were real inoculations or some kind of experimentation to which we were being subjected. As a nurse in the infirmary, I was present when people lined up to get their injections. I kept myself busy and moved to the end of the line, blending in with those who already had been inoculated. That's how I managed to avoid being inoculated. Many people got typhus following these injections and the disease was more widespread than ever. At this time, I was ordered to copy a German poster, which showed a skull being invaded by a louse. The text said: *Jude Seuche* (Jew Pestilence). It was intended to warn Germans to stay away from Jews because they were carriers of disease.

As an additional precautionary measure, all prisoners, Jews and non-Jews alike, were ordered to take cold showers and wash their clothing in a disinfecting liquid. They had to put on their clothing while it was still wet. Because people were already sick and weak, this additional cruelty caused several dozen deaths within a few days.

By this time, February, 1945, work in the factory had slowed down. Near the factory were many railway tracks, intended for shipping tanks and armament to the front. The number of tanks being transported out dropped dramatically. More and more, the tracks were used for trains carrying wounded soldiers home from the front. There was also a lot of sabotage within the factory. The French, in particular, were first-class saboteurs. They would drop a nail into the machines and the whole operation would come to a halt. The Germans would take people out and give them murderous beatings. Some of the German civilian supervisors dropped hints that the war was not going well for Germany.

Evenings in Zschachwitz were monotonous. Gradually, the first-aid station became a kind of social club. In addition to those of us who worked there, a number of non-Jewish Kapos would drop in during the evening. The oldest was Ferdinand, a German criminal prisoner who was extremely well read. There was Fritz, a skinny, skeleton-like homosexual who frequently raped newly arrived teenagers. There was Paul from Hamburg, a tall, broadly built man with deep-set green eyes and protruding teeth. He boasted that he had killed his in-laws and other relatives. At the same time, he frequently spoke about justice and morality, as if to justify his deeds. Additional personalities at these evening discussions included Anatol, a Russian officer who spoke German and was deeply respected—and feared—by the other Russians and Ukrainians. There were some Italians, Greeks, an Englishman named Cliff, and a member of the Polish diplomatic service who had served in Germany. Finally, there was Kurt Buchenholz, a Jewish engineer from Berlin, a man of intellect, dignity, and warmth.

The discussions in the evening covered every topic, including politics. We had the sense that the Germans foresaw the defeat of Germany and were trying to draw closer to us in case they needed us as allies later on. Some of the Kapos expressed the desire to escape and Ferdinand actually did so.

The prisoners slept on the top floor of the vast hall, which could only be reached by huge elevators. Here wooden bunks had been constructed. As the Allies moved closer, and the air raid sirens sounded, we were taken down to the basement shelter until it was safe to go up again. But after a while, as air raids became more frequent, they discontinued this practice and left us, locked in, on the top floor. We were convinced that they did this to blackmail the Allies into not bombing the plant since, by doing so, they would kill many prisoners. The first-aid station and the morgue, however, were transferred from the top floor to the basement where they remained until the end. For a while, several of us working in the station were allowed to sleep there as well. Then, for reasons which were never explained, we were ordered to sleep with the other prisoners on the top floor.

About ten in the evening on February 12, 1945, the sirens began to wail, announcing an air raid. This was nothing unusual. It had been going on for weeks. We had learned simply to ignore the air raids and sleep through the night. Anyway, we were locked in and not permitted to go to the shelter in the basement.

But that night things were different. Soon after the sirens sounded, the sky was lit up by flares dropped from the planes. The Allies were bombing Dresden. Bombs began raining down on the factory complex as well. Around us buildings went up in flames. Then the bombs began hitting our building. The panic was immense. We were locked in and faced certain death. The explosions shattered the huge glass windows of the sleeping hall and prisoners began climbing out the windows and down the drainpipes running down the side of the building. Some lost their grip and fell to their deaths. Others began throwing themselves frantically against the huge steel door—which was locked—and the wall that led to

Miag Werke, Zschachwitz near Dresden before bombardment, 1945.
Source unknown

the outside corridor and staircases. After a while, the wall and the doors gave way; many prisoners died in the ensuing stampede.

I had two friends that I was not going to leave behind in the burning building: Arthur Meissner, a Warsaw Jew and a former sergeant in the Polish army, and Lichtenstein, another Warsaw Jew. They were both ill and could hardly move. I dragged them with me and was carried along by the mob. Suddenly we found ourselves in an empty stairwell. Somehow, the crowd had gone to the left and we three were alone. Lichtenstein, though weak, managed to walk, but Meissner was completely immobilized by a thrombosis in his right leg and I had to carry him.

We made our way down the stairs and found ourselves on the main manufacturing floor of the building. The vast hall was in ruins and deserted. Trains loaded with Tiger 52 tanks stood motionless on the tracks. We crawled under the trains toward the exit. There were no guards about, everything was silent except for the immense fires that burned all around. In the distance, the sky was ablaze with the fire that was destroying Dresden.

When we got out of the building, we crossed the barbed wire surrounding the factory and the tracks on which burning trains were standing. We continued toward an open field, hearing and seeing other prisoners running in various directions. After about a half hour we reached a highway. We knew we were in the heart of Germany. We saw Germans dragging all sorts of wagons and carriages filled with their belongings and crying children. To see Germans in such a situation was something entirely new to us.

A middle-aged German escaping with his family approached us and asked us how close the Russians were. Germans were particularly terrified of the Russians because their propaganda had told them that the Russians would murder them all. Though we had no idea where the Russians were, we told him that they were in Heidenau, a few kilometers away. This terrified him even more. Seeing from our clothing that we were prisoners, he fell on his knees and begged us to stay with him in his nearby house. We would receive food and shelter and all we had to do was to speak up for him when the Russians showed up.

We refused the offer because we were afraid. We were escaped prisoners and we did not know what to do. We roamed the fields aimlessly until daybreak when we were surrounded by large numbers of German civilians and some SA (*Sturmabteilung*—Brown shirts) men with guns. An alarm had gone out that fifteen hundred prisoners had escaped and they were assigned to round us up. The prisoners did not resist because we knew we were in the heartland of Germany and there was nowhere to hide. At the same time, we did not have the feeling that this roundup was very dangerous. It was clear that liberation was near and the attitude of the German civilians reflected it.

Within several hours, most of the surviving prisoners were back in custody and were handed over to the SS. When we were counted it turned out that over one hundred prisoners were missing. They had been killed or injured in the raid and in the panic accompanying it. The SS men who took control of us were, if anything, more vicious than before. The imminent defeat of Germany did not improve their behavior. They were furious over the raid and took their anger out on us. They kept us in the ruins of the former factory and put us to work cleaning it up, a hopeless task if ever there was one. We received practically no food, only thin soup.

We gathered the corpses. Some people had been sick already and had died of their illnesses. Others had been killed during the raid: they had jumped, or fallen, or been trampled to death during the bombing. Caskets were supplied and two bodies were placed in each casket. They were then loaded on trucks and taken to a nearby field where huge ditches had been dug.

I returned to the infirmary. It was a shambles. Someone had ransacked it during the air raid. I checked the medical supply closet. Under a pile of various supplies, I had hidden the Waltham pocket watch that had belonged to my father's cousin, Flamm. It was gone.

On the evening of March 6, 1945, Simon Sagh celebrated the birthday of his daughter, Eva. Eva had gone to the United States to study before the war and fortunately remained there. It was just the three of us: Simon, Alexander, and I. We drank a toast to her health and he told me that, just before being deported, he had learned that she had married in the United States and her married name was Kershaw. He also told me that she had given birth to a boy. He hoped that the child had been circumcised and that he would leave behind him a Jewish grandchild.

Shortly after this, the German district doctor came down with typhus. Simon was summoned for a consultation. I do not know what happened to the doctor. At about the same time, Alexander came down with typhus. He was sick for about two weeks. His brother Simon, aided by Dr. Josef Mandel, did all they could. One night Alexander had a very high fever and Simon gave him a spinal tap to relieve the pressure on his brain. It was no use. About twenty-four hours later, at 3:00 A.M., Alexander died. That morning, all remaining prisoners in the camp were lined up with their caps off, and the body of Alexander Sagh was carried on a stretcher in front of them throughout the entire length of the complex. Simon, crying uncontrollably, held on to me as we walked behind the body of his brother, reciting *Kaddish*. The body was taken by truck to be buried with several other bodies. I do not know exactly where he was buried. I was told that he was placed in a mass grave not far from the factory.

Simon was heartbroken. About a week or so later, he too fell ill with typhus. He had an extremely high fever and felt that his life was ebbing away. He told me that he knew this was the end and handed me his lower denture, which had some gold teeth. He blessed me and prayed that I would survive. He asked me to find his daughter, Eva, tell her his tragic story, and deliver the dentures to her.

Now air raids occurred frequently. Hundreds of planes flew overheard; it sounded like earthquakes, like the world was coming to an end. Over and over, we were forced out of the factory into a nearby field where we were told to disperse, or herded into air raid shelters. After several more air raid alarms, we were told that we were being evacuated. First, a selection took place. The sick and weak were thrown into trucks and taken away. It was clear that they were going to be killed. I shoved several sick persons under their beds to help them escape the selection. (One of these was a young Pole, Jerzy Grochowski, a sign painter, who had been captured during the Polish uprising in Warsaw in 1944. He survived.)

The rest of us were lined up. Each person was given one slice of bread. The prisoners, accompanied by guards, were marched off toward the south. Tauscher, the SS commandant of the camp, provided one open truck for the sick—Simon among them—who had not been sent away in the selection. Tauscher also gave me a canister of water and some cubes of sugar for Simon. I believe these were gestures of gratitude for the abortion Simon had performed on Tauscher's girl friend. Another prisoner and I were assigned as medics on the truck.

Our destination was the concentration camp in Leitmeritz, a town ninety kilometers south of Dresden, in the Sudetenland. The trip took all day, from early morning to late at night. The truck broke down several times and had to be repaired. The landscape we passed through was beautiful: serene, lush, and architecturally fascinating. It had not been touched by the war at all, though we noticed very few young men about. During our stop in various villages, a number of German women looked at us with bewilderment. At one point, one of the prisoners fell off the truck and cut his forehead badly. A German woman noticed this and came out with a jug of water. The SS man guarding us knocked the jug out of her hand with his rifle and told her to get the hell out of there.

When we arrived in Leitmeritz late at night on April 24, 1945, we found a large concentration camp in chaos. The truck was met by several medics and Dr. Orlik, a Jewish doctor from Prague. Before the stretcher cases were taken away, I pointed Simon out to Dr. Orlik and he promised to do the best he could for him. The rest of us were taken for delousing. By this time, the only personal effects I still had with me were some family photographs, my father's razor, and Simon's golden dentures. After undressing, I approached a German Kapo, a BV, and pleaded with him to hold my photographs for me. He accepted them and told me to pick them up the next day in his barrack, which I did. I never saw this man before or afterward. He must have understood what such pictures meant to a prisoner. But I also had to hide the gold denture. I straightened it out, broke it into two pieces and hid them in my anus. While my mouth and ears were examined, my anus was not and so I saved the dentures. However, in so doing, I injured my rectum and suffered for days. I held my father's razor in my hand and this, too, was not noticed. These are the only objects that survived the war with me.

The next day, about seven in the morning, I visited Simon in the camp "hospital." He was unconscious and clearly dying. When I returned at one in the afternoon, he was close to death. About half an hour after my arrival, Simon Sagh died. His body, along with several others, was carried to the crematorium.

My first morning in Leitmeritz, I was awakened by a vicious kick in my kidneys administered by Fritz, the homosexual Kapo from Zschachwitz who had frequently participated in our evening discussions in the infirmary. I looked at him in bewilderment and he bellowed: "It makes no difference, you dirty dog." The morning lineup was even more frightening. The usual screams, beatings, and kicks had a macabre twist: they were accompanied by music. As we were standing in the lineup being beaten, I heard strains of music coming from an orchestra of mostly gentile prisoners in terrible shape, dressed in standard striped uniforms with identification numbers, and playing instruments. They stood to the right of the main gate through which we had to pass, and played German marches as we marched to work in the stone quarries. The rhythm of the marches mixed with the rhythm of the whips as the guards hit us.

In the quarries we had to break pieces of rock from the exposed cliffs using picks, crowbars, and shovels. This was back-breaking work and had no value whatsoever. The stones were never used for anything. It was simply a method of killing people a little more slowly than the gas chambers. Prisoners told me that people did not last long in the quarries. In addition to those who died from exertion combined with malnutrition, on any given day the Kapos would kill a few by throwing them over the cliff or strangling them.

When I first arrived in Leitmeritz, Jews and gentiles were together in the barracks. Soon after, however, they began to separate the Jews from the gentiles. One Polish gentile prisoner wanted to help me and suggested that I stay with him and not join the Jewish groups. At first I did so, believing that this might indeed be safer. With me was David Grynberg, the scholar of Hebrew literature who had been with me in Okęcie and Budzyń. However, we were still in danger because any gentile who knew who we were could have reported us. After two days, Grynberg and I rejoined the Jewish group. We did not have the energy to continue this game. We felt that we belonged with the other Jews and were resigned to sharing their fate.

21

They kept us in Leitmeritz about six days. One morning, toward the end of April, we were ordered to start marching again. We marched a distance of about seven kilometers, and arrived, exhausted, in Theresienstadt in the afternoon.

Theresienstadt was different from the camps I had known until then. It was a fortress with huge stone buildings and tremendous archways. There were railroad tracks, though I did not see any trains, any transports.

While I was there, I knew nothing about it having been a "model camp," which the Germans displayed to the Red Cross inspection teams to prove that their treatment of prisoners was humane. I heard that, at one time, all kinds of cultural activities had been conducted in the camp, but by the time I got there, everything was in chaos. The streets were empty, and I did not see many people, although I found out later that there were thirty-six thousand people in the camp.

Most of those I did see were elderly, who had been deported from Germany and other Western countries. I saw no gentiles in the camp. The inmates were either Jewish or part Jewish. Some were Jewish converts to Christianity.

The strangest thing about Theresienstadt was its silent atmosphere of terror. It was very quiet, like a dying city. There was a dead stillness over everything. People huddled together in little groups. I witnessed no beatings there. The food was miserable, as bad as it had been in any of the camps.

My group was housed in the *Hamburger Kaserne,* a huge three-story building containing large halls with sixty to seventy bunks in each. I was assigned to a room with only seven other prisoners.

We had been told way back in Budzyń that the Russians were approaching and the Allies were winning. But we were still waiting for deliverance, and we no longer believed any of these stories. However, the SS presence seemed to be diminishing and most of the administration was taken over by the prisoners. I volunteered to work in the hospital where there was much typhus and tuberculosis, and few doctors and little medicine. Every day people died.

At Theresienstadt, I was near the end of my rope. In the camps, I had lived in an atmosphere of unrelenting maximum tension. Constant movement, constant activity: killing, shooting, beating, yelling. Suddenly, after this storm of events, I was brought into a thundering stillness. It was like coming into a morgue. The quiet and the dark, looming architecture felt like the end of the world. There was a sort of apathy mixed with fear of the unknown. Then I was told by a number of inmates, including Jo Spier, the foremost Dutch political cartoonist (who had a studio in Theresienstadt and was permitted to work on assignments given to him by the Germans), that this place, which was so quiet, was a place of final destiny. From here, I was told, the trains went straight into the unknown.

I was exhausted. I was depressed. Around me, people began wondering whether they might actually be liberated, and what they would do afterward. I began to wonder myself. Where could I go, anyway? There was nothing left, no one left. I knew, subconsciously, that I would not find anybody. I could not envision my father, my brothers, my sister, surviving after I saw them practically dead. The world was completely empty, physically, spiritually. Returning to it would be like going into a void. I had the sense that even if, miraculously, I were to survive, I would have to ask myself what the purpose of my survival was. I felt restless, wondering, what's next?

What brought me back to myself was the arrival of the Russians. At five o'clock on the morning of May 8, 1945, we heard artillery and machine-gun fire. There was the rumbling of tanks and then the street filled with jeeps full of Russian soldiers. Soon there were hundreds of them, men and women. There was tremendous commotion and confusion. The Russian soldiers were screaming "*Svoboda!*" (Freedom!) Most of the prisoners reacted with apathy, though a few were in the mood to celebrate. One climbed on top of a tank, lost his grip, and fell under the tread of the tank.

The Russians immediately began distributing bread and setting up baths right in the middle of the yards. Soon the medical teams began arriving. Their attitude was deeply compassionate. They knew of our suffering and treated us with great gentleness and care. They deserve all the credit for their humanity. I had the feeling that we were reunited with members of the family. My frozen feelings began to thaw, little by little. After a number of days, very slowly, I felt myself start to come to life, and I began to accept all these sensations, slowly, slowly.

Loudspeakers broadcast the message that we were to be very careful about what we ate. We were not to eat too much, and should especially stay away from fats, because our digestive systems needed time to get used to normal food. From their experience in liberating other camps, the Russians had seen the effects of undisciplined eating on starving prisoners. Nevertheless, hundreds of people died. Some would have died anyway, no matter what they did, but others might have lived had they been able to control their urge to eat too much. I befriended the head of the medical unit, Dr. Yesayef from Moscow, and his chief nurse, Alexandra, a young woman in her twenties from Leningrad. As a sergeant with the medical corps, Alexandra, or Shura, as we called her, had gone through the entire campaign from Stalingrad all the way to the end. She was an angel. She moved about all the patients with boiled farina. She told us, "We don't even give this to our own sick soldiers. We brought it for you." She pleaded with me and with others to eat only what they prepared, namely farina, barley, and boiled potatoes. They would not permit us to eat anything cold or uncooked. I stayed on this diet for several weeks before they added various foods gradually. For a long time, they did not permit us to eat meat or fish. Fortunately, I had no trouble on this diet and before long, I was feeling much better.

They also immediately quarantined the camp. In order to leave the area, you had to submit to delousing and a medical exam. It was almost three months before the Russian authorities began to dissolve the camp. Until then, Russian military sentries made sure no one left the camp. The Russians questioned many prisoners about their experiences in the camp and documented their testimonies for their official records.

Several days after the liberation, I volunteered to work

with the medical unit as a male nurse. We gathered together all the sick, the disabled. A number of Jewish doctors who had been in hiding in Prague and had been liberated by the Soviets joined us. In addition, hundreds of Czech non-Jewish volunteers from Prague appeared in response to a call that Theresienstadt had been liberated and there were prisoners in distress. These included doctors and nurses, as well as civilians, women who did excellent work in cleaning and feeding the survivors. Some patients began to realize that they were free, and their will to live began to assert itself. In many cases, however, it was no use. Though they had lived long enough to see the enemy defeated, they could not defeat their illnesses, their agony. Some lost their minds as their last resistance crumbled. Others died of typhus, dysentery, tuberculosis, or malnutrition. One of these last victims was *Der Geyler Mordche,* the redheaded Kapo from Budzyń who had saved many lives with his ferocious screaming. He died from tuberculosis following the liberation. For him and many others, liberation came too late.

About a week after liberation, I left the camp with a group of prisoners to visit the surrounding area. We were simply curious to see the outside world. The towns seemed very quiet because the Germans kept out of sight, hiding in their houses. They were deathly afraid of the Russians. We knocked at one house and, when there was no answer, began to break down the door. Suddenly, a German appeared and offered us anything he had as long as we did not harm him. We entered his cellar and found it well stocked with food of every description. We helped ourselves to some of it and left.

By the end of June, word got around that we would soon be sent home. Some of the Jews from Western Europe, particularly the Christian converts and those who had intermarried, looked forward to being reunited with their loved ones.

213

There were even some reunions among these groups in Theresienstadt. My friend Kurt Buchenholz, the engineer from Berlin who worked with me as a male nurse in the infirmary in Zschachwitz, found his wife Pauline in Theresienstadt. (They moved to the United States where he lived until his death in 1991.)

But, to most of the Polish Jewish survivors, the thought of going home was very painful. Most of us were almost certain that we were the only survivors in our families. We had no one to return to.

The Russian authorities began to release groups of prisoners. Others had already left on their own, without waiting for the official clearance. Dr. Yesayef urged me to wait a little, until things settled down all over Europe. He invited me to come home with him to Moscow. His son, he told me, was finishing medical school. He would adopt me as his second son, and I could pursue my career in fine art in the Soviet Union. A different viewpoint was expressed by a Jew, a major in the Soviet Army. He took me aside one evening, and said to me, in Yiddish, "Meshke, if you have a chance, go to your uncle in America. I don't think life in the Soviet Union is for you." I listened to all these different viewpoints. In the meantime, I was in no hurry to leave, to go back to Poland. And yet, I had a very strong desire to go back to the soil, look at the place once more, and relive it all again. I couldn't pull myself away from it completely. It was as though a magnet was pulling me to go back and take one last look. I knew no one was waiting for me there. I was almost sure that Pesach was not alive anymore because my aunt's brother-in-law, Leib Drajer, had seen him in the ghetto when the final uprising broke out. (Leib Drajer died in Majdanek, a short while after passing this news on to me.) But I still nurtured the tiniest hope that maybe Shlomo or Esther had managed to sneak away somehow, because I had no direct evidence that anyone had actually seen them die.

On July 19, 1945, it was my turn to start my journey back to the place where I had once had a home. The members of the medical unit, with whom I was on very warm terms, made a beautiful farewell celebration—with cabbage and herring, bread and vodka—for those of us who had volunteered at the hospital. Then they put us on a passenger train heading for Poland.

There were trains heading in all directions. All returning refugees were given passes entitling us to cross the border into Poland, a suit, some underwear, and some food.

In addition, I carried with me the following personal items:

1. I had my father's tiny razor, which I had always kept with me in one of my pockets.

2. I still had the little red makeshift cardboard folder containing the original photographs of my family. I had saved it a thousand times since Okęcie. I had kept it in my pockets, hidden it under the boards on which I slept. I had stuffed it into cracks of the walls along which I worked, and buried it, wrapped in rags, in the sand by the barracks if the weather was dry. On several occasions, by some miracle, it was saved for me by others: twice by Feix's mascot "Borscht" in Budzyń, and once by the criminal Kapo, the BV, in Leitmeritz.

3. In Budzyń, I had asked Eljowicz, the photographer, to make a reduction of these original family photographs. The miniature he produced measured 1¾ inches by 1½ inches. I framed it in a little piece of aluminum and wore it around my neck on a piece of string. Because it vaguely resembled an army dogtag, it was overlooked during searches. I was wearing it when I was liberated.

4. I had Simon Sagh's golden dentures.

5. And I had one thing which was restored to me: one day, a group of Jews raided a few apartments in a nearby German town. When they returned to Theresienstadt, one of them handed me something: a drafting set. I accepted it as symbolic reparation for the one that had been stolen from me in those last few seconds before I was loaded onto the cattle car at the Warsaw *Umschlagplatz*.

The train left Theresienstadt in the late afternoon, heading for Poland. Traveling slowly, with many stops, we reached the border the next morning. We were questioned and searched by Polish border guards, who prepared new identity papers for us. I was told that the Polish Red Cross offered some small assistance to returning refugees, so I went there. There was more paperwork. I gave my name to the woman filling out the papers: Mieczysław (the Polish version of Morris) Wyszogród. It was Polish enough; Wyszogród, after all, is the name of a Polish city north of Warsaw. Without any hesitation, she wrote "Roman Catholic" in the space for religion. Maybe it didn't cross her mind that she would come across any Jews. In any event, she gave me one hundred zlotys for the trip, some bread, and a piece of herring, and I resumed the journey. I traveled with a fellow inmate from Theresienstadt, Mr. Sznaj, a tailor returning to his home town, Łódź.

We arrived in Warsaw toward evening on July 20, 1945. The train could not enter the city because the railway stations had been destroyed, so it stopped at a makeshift station on the outskirts of the city, and we disembarked.

22

There was a shed next to the railroad tracks, where representatives of the Polish Red Cross were distributing coffee, bread, and marmalade. After eating, I fell asleep on the ground near the shed, under the open sky. Suddenly I felt a boot nudge me in the middle of my back. I opened my eyes and saw some silhouettes with flashlights. It was a patrol of Russian military police, conducting a routine check. They looked through my papers, apologized for waking me up, and wished me a peaceful night. There were many refugees sleeping in the open. It was a beautiful night. The sky was covered with stars. I went back to sleep.

In the morning, I did not immediately start walking into Warsaw. I was afraid of what awaited me. I did not believe I would meet any Jews I had known before the war. I just hung around the shed where some food was available, waiting until Sznaj caught his train to Łódź. I don't remember seeing any

Jews there, just military personnel, people in the process of repatriation or on their way into the city.

Toward evening, I noticed a group of Polish soldiers, among them several officers. One of them, a lieutenant, looked Jewish. I approached him and asked, "*Amkho?*" (One of us?) He seemed delighted, answered that he was and embraced me. We began exchanging information about ourselves. "Where are you from?" he asked. I told him, "From Hell. And you?" He was also from Warsaw, a member of the prominent Graf family who had built their fortune dealing in metals and had been well known before the war for their wealth and philanthropy. He had spent the war in the Soviet Union attached to a Polish unit fighting with the Red Army. He was returning from Berlin and looking forward to his discharge. Like me, he had no home to return to. We spent most of the night talking and in the morning he left.

That morning, I started my trip into reality. It was a beautiful morning. I started walking into Warsaw, toward my home, my little satchel thrown over my shoulder. The destruction in the center of the city was beyond belief, although the main streets had already been cleared of rubble and trucks and cars were moving. The first person I met was Mr. Brown, a black dancer and jazz musician who had been a friend of my father's. Originally from French Africa and one of only three black musicians in Warsaw, he performed in the city's top cabarets. I identified myself to him and he remembered me. He asked about my father. He invited me up to his house to wash up and rest but I told him that I would visit him some other time.

About ten minutes later, I came across Professor Szumański, a professor of Polish history and literature from high school. He told me that he had saved a number of Jews but I did not know whether or not to believe him. Next, I saw

Kazimierz Kamiński, another Christian musician who had known my father and had visited us frequently. He asked what he could do to help me and invited me to his home. Here was another family welcoming me, but not the family I wanted to see. I thanked him for the invitation.

Then I started walking toward the ghetto. When I had last seen it in May, 1943, most of the buildings were burned-out shells. Now there was nothing left standing at all. The entire area of the ghetto was a sea of rubble, just bricks stretching toward the horizon. I oriented myself by the Pawiak prison, which, though in ruins, could still be recognized. The one remaining tower of the Saint Augustine Church served as another orientation point.

The area was totally dead. There was no one there but me. Opposite the church was a burned-out skeleton of a building. There was still a bit of the balcony left, and the windows. This was 32 Dzielna Street, the building in which my grandparents had lived, and where I was born and had spent the early years of my childhood. I leaned against the brick fence of the church and stared at the ruins. Memories of my childhood passed through my mind: my fifth birthday when our friend Yossl played the fiddle to make me and my parents happy, the parades of children marching through the streets. I remembered playing in the churchyard, and taking shortcuts through it to school on snowy winter days, and the elderly priest who sometimes gave us candy. I remembered the church chapel where we would sneak in to see the bodies prepared for funerals, and the music of Chopin's march. Now the only sound I heard was the wind blowing through the leaves on some trees that had remained standing and were now in bloom.

I stood there for a while, then I dragged myself along Dzielna Street toward Smocza Street. The streets were not there but I knew where I was because, before the war, each corner had had a cylindrical electrical transformer on which posters and announcements were pasted. Some of these still remained, dark and rusted, and they served as my guide. Now they bore messages scribbled on them in brick chalk by returning survivors, announcing that they were alive. At the corner of what used to be Pawia and Smocza Streets, one of these transformers still stood in the midst of a huge pile of rubble. I picked up a piece of brick and wrote on it in Polish: "Mojżesz Wyszogród, Pawia 48, returned. Information: Jewish Committee, 5 Szeroka Street, Praga." I hoped that someone would see it and contact me.

There was only a vague indication of a street. I walked around for a while trying to find 48 Pawia Street, our last home in the ghetto. I was finally able to locate the spot where it had stood by judging the distance from a manhole. I found pieces of our wrought-iron balcony in the rubble. I found the little metal sign, Pawia 35, from the house across from mine. I thought of taking it, then dropped it. It belonged here. I sat down. It seemed to me that I could hear the voices of my mother and my father, my brothers and sister, the voices of my friends, the sound of musical instruments. The noisy screams, curses, and blessings of merchants on the streets. I don't know how long I sat there.

Suddenly my attention was attracted by a noise coming from the ruins. It seemed to me for a second that the earth was opening. I jumped up in fear. It was an old woman, dressed in black, who had appeared as if from nowhere, scavenging in the rubble. The story had spread that Jews had buried treasures in the ghetto and, from time to time, people still came to hunt for them. She frightened me, and I decided to leave this place.

I stood up and started walking toward Praga, a section of

Pawia and Smocza Streets

Pawia 48, Warsaw, 1945
Author on the ruins
of his home
Photos: Jan Roguski

Warsaw on the other side of the Vistula River, taking the same
route along which I had been marched to the *Umschlagplatz*.
On the way, I passed the prewar military prison on Gęsia
Street where thousands of Jews had been killed by the Gestapo. The French and Greek Jews who had been brought in
by the Gestapo to reduce the remains of the ghetto to rubble

had been imprisoned here as well. The prison seemed to be functioning and a sentry motioned me away. I continued toward the Marshal Józef Piłsudski School of Graphic Arts at 2 Konwiktorska Street. The building was intact, and the old superintendent, Mr. Wierzbowski, recognized and greeted me warmly. I went inside and was received by the new director of the school, my former teacher, Professor Bolesław Penciak. He was amazed and shocked to see me. I had the feeling that he found the reunion painful; maybe he felt guilty. The last time I had gone to see him, in 1941, he had told me that he was sorry but he couldn't help me, had handed me some bread—which I refused—and closed the door. Now he invited me in and offered me some coffee, bread, and jam, and this time I accepted. I told him of my experiences after being deported from Warsaw. He explained that he could not let me into his house back then because he had been involved in underground activities and had been afraid to jeopardize them, and his wife and child. He seemed ready to do anything for me now but I told him that all I wanted was a copy of my diploma, which he promptly provided.

Praga, where the Jewish Committee was located, was mostly intact, although some buildings had been damaged during the war. A group of survivors milled about the office on Szeroka Street. The committee was compiling lists of survivors, and after registering myself on one of these, I looked through them with great anxiety. I recognized no names.

I received a small amount of money, enough for one day's food, and was sent to an address on Targowa Street for lodging. When I got there, I found a partially destroyed building. Only the basement and first floor were habitable, and all the apartments were already occupied. As I tried to decide what to do next, a man emerged from a nearby basement and looked at me. Instantly, he threw his arms around me. It was

Samuel Cylich, a childhood friend who had lived in our building. He had survived the war in the Soviet Union and now ran a small radio repair shop in the basement from which he had just emerged. He immediately invited me to stay with him and his wife Ruth, and I did, for a few months. I escaped death one more time, when the building we lived in, which had been partially destroyed during the war, collapsed completely. Two sisters who had survived Auschwitz were killed. The Cylichs and I were not in the building when it happened.

I stayed in Warsaw for one year. I kept trying to make contact with any remaining members of my family. A friend, Henry Edelsbourgh, helped me send a telegram to the United States to the Committee for Polish Jews, asking them to include my name in the lists of survivors that appeared in the major Yiddish newspapers of the day, *The Forward* and the *Morgen Journal*. What happened next I later learned from my cousins in New York. Their father, my uncle Mendel, returned from the synagogue at the end of Yom Kippur, picked up the paper, and read: "Moshe Mordechai (Morris Wyszogrod) is alive, the only survivor, looking for families Blaifeder, Gershberg, Lasko, in Brooklyn." My uncle started screaming and collapsed and his family had to revive him. The next thing I knew, I received a telegram: "Very happy to hear from you. Help on the way. Your Uncle Mendel and Family. God Bless You." We began writing back and forth. I received forty-nine letters from my uncle in the two years that were to pass before we were reunited.

Toward the end of 1945, I joined the staff of the American Jewish Joint Distribution Committee (JDC) in Warsaw. Shortly before starting to work for them, I joined two Russian military surgeons on a trip to Berlin. Dr. Feinberg was a Jew from Kiev, and Dr. Fiodor Pavlovich Ishchenko was the personal physician to Soviet General Rokosofsky. Cylich had introduced me to them at the Soviet military field hospital in Praga shortly after my return to Warsaw. I prepared graphs and statistical drawings for their research projects and we became very friendly. Now they were being sent to Berlin. They suggested that I go along with them to see whether it would be easier to proceed to the West from there.

They procured a Soviet military uniform without insignia for me and papers that certified me as an interpreter assigned to accompany them. We left Warsaw on the morning of December 31, 1945, and arrived on the outskirts of Berlin on New Year's Eve. We spent the evening in a German beer hall. It was very hard for me to see Germans celebrating and having a good time. When I told my friends how I felt, they replied that the Germans had been conquered and I should consider myself their master.

The next day was more gratifying. Berlin was badly damaged, although the work of cleaning up had progressed nicely, far more so than in Warsaw. Together with my liberators, I visited the Brandenburg Gate, from which the flags of the four occupying powers now flew. Nearby, the Reichstag building lay in ruins. After everything I had suffered, this gave me some satisfaction, but not enough. The Germans seemed terrified of the Russian uniform. However crowded the U-Bahn subway trains were, whenever we entered one, the crowd drew back in fear, leaving plenty of empty space around us.

Dr. Ishchenko accompanied me to the JDC office in Berlin to discuss my options for getting to the United States. One alternative was to go to a Displaced Persons (DP) camp in Germany, but I never wanted to step on German soil again. In addition, the prospects of immigration to the United States from there were not clear. Because I had relatives in America with whom I had already established contact, the JDC representatives thought that my visa application would probably be processed faster from Warsaw. They advised me to return and await my visa there. I decided to take their advice and, after traveling some more with my Russian friends, I returned to Warsaw.

I worked for the JDC in Warsaw until the summer of 1946. The JDC did whatever it could to support the returning survivors. It acted as the representative of American Jewry in healing the wounds of the survivors. It distributed clothing and food and established medical facilities.

Many survivors wanted to leave Poland and build new lives elsewhere. Some tried to immigrate to Palestine, even though the only way to do that was by illegal means. Others, like me, were waiting for visas to the United States. And there were some who believed, despite all that Polish Jewry had been through, that it was still possible to reestablish some kind of limited Jewish life on Polish soil. This illusion was shattered by the killings that occurred as soon as the tiny numbers of surviving Jews tried to return to their homes. They were met with hostility from neighbors reluctant to part with Jewish property they had obtained. This came to a climax in a pogrom in Kielce on July 4, 1946. Forty-two Jews, including pregnant women and children, were murdered by Poles in connection with a blood libel. I was sent by the JDC to Kielce and saw the building, dripping with blood, in which the murders had occurred. This proved to almost all Jews, except fervent Jewish Communists, that Jewish life in Poland had no future.

One day, a man came into the JDC office where I worked. It was Zaleski, the man for whom I had counterfeited documents in the ghetto. The last time I had seen him was in 1942, just after my mother had been taken away. I had been running around the streets of the ghetto desperately trying to find someone to help me. One of the people I met then was Zaleski. He had looked at me. He must have seen in my face the destruction. He took twenty zlotys from his pocket and gave them to me.

Now we met again. He had somehow survived on the Aryan side, but when I asked him how, all he said was, "Well, it was tough." I hoped to sit down with him, find out the truth about who he was, what he had done during the war. But he left Warsaw, giving me an address, a post office box in Caracas, Venezuela, which I still have. I never saw him again.

Shortly before I left Poland, I found my cousin Abraham Joseph Wyszegrod, son of my father's oldest brother Hirsh Baer from Lublin. He was the only one of his family—parents and six siblings—still alive. He had survived in the Soviet Union. He knocked on my door at five o'clock on the morning of July 20, the day I was leaving Poland. He had traveled all night by train from Stettin, where he now lived, fearful of possible attacks by members of the *Armia Krajowa* (AK, the Polish Home Army), who were known to pull Jews off the trains and kill them. We spent the day together, reminiscing about our past and exchanging stories. He was among the group of friends and coworkers who came to see me off at the Warsaw railway station that evening. (In 1950, he made his way to Israel where he now lives, with his wife, his children, and six grandchildren.)

I left Warsaw for Paris on July 20, 1946. I stayed in Paris for about a year, working for the JDC and attending French and English evening classes. One of my coworkers at the JDC was a lovely young woman named Lillian. One day, as a group of us sat in a café on our lunch break, someone addressed her as "Mademoiselle Scherschneider."

226

I said, "Wait a minute. Lillian, is your name Scher-schneider?"

"Yes."

"What is your father's name?"

"My father's name is Bernard."

I asked, "What is his profession?"

She said, "He manufactures clothing."

"Where did he come from?"

"From Warsaw."

I said, "Call your father, and ask him if he remembers Chaim Boruch Wyszogrod from his young years in Warsaw." She came back to the table moved to tears, and said, "My father wants to see you immediately. He remembers your father well."

They made a reception for me on Saturday in their home, in a nice section of Paris, not far from the Place de la Republique. They sat me at the head of the table, drank a *l'chaim* in my honor, and Berele told the story of how my father had helped him—and his five sisters—leave Poland. They all survived in the Vichy zone (although by the time I met him, one of the sisters had died).

He wanted to give me a generous gift to help me as I moved to America. I thanked him but would not accept it. I felt he did not owe me anything, my father wouldn't have liked me to be paid for what he did, and I had a certain pride. Instead, I let him take me to a big department store in Paris and treat me to three new ties, "one for everyday, one for Shabbat, and one for when you meet your relatives." Then we said goodbye. (I kept in touch with them for a while. Lillian got married and lives in Lyons, France.)

I left for the United States on August 9, 1947, on a student visa to study advertising design at Pratt Institute in

Brooklyn, New York. I was fulfilling my promise to my mother to be reunited with her brother, Mendel Blaifeder, who had left Poland for the United States in 1929 with his wife Faige and their three children. On August 19, 1947, I sailed past the Statue of Liberty into New York harbor, to begin a new life in the New World.

Epilogue

As the SS Marine Jumper docked at Pier 32 in New York harbor, I looked down from the deck and recognized my Uncle Mendel. He looked up, our eyes met and filled with tears. He tossed a candy up to me, which I caught.

I disembarked and we embraced. His face was pale, full of pain, and so was mine. It was hard to believe that we were touching each other. It was eighteen years since I saw him leave for the Golden Land with his family. With him at the pier were his wife, Faige, and his children, Morris, who had served in the American Army during the war, Martin, and Esther. They took me home. Above the door hung a big sign that my uncle had calligraphed: "Welcome to our home, dear Morris." People began arriving—my aunt Faige's relatives, friends, neighbors—all asking questions: how it was, how I survived, if I had met any of their friends and relatives. My uncle cried endlessly, touched me and kissed me over and over.

The pain he suffered over the loss of his family ended his life two short years later, in 1949.

In my first weeks in the United States, I fulfilled my vow to Simon Sagh: I met his daughter, Eva Kershaw, her husband, Murray, who had been a fighter pilot in the United States Air Force during the war, and their small son, David. In an emotional meeting, I handed Eva her father's dentures. She broke down in tears and embraced me. "You are my brother," she said.

Soon after my arrival, I started my studies at Pratt Institute. I received an enthusiastic welcome from the Dean James C. Boudreau, the professors, and my fellow classmates, many of whom were veterans of the United States Army. Some of those who opened their hearts and homes to me were Rodolfo Edmundo Urias and his wife Artemisa, Edward Wallant, Irene Murray Callaghan, Thomas Ruzicka, Jonathan Trout, and George Tscherny. Their heartwarming reception added to my fervent desire to succeed and build a life and a future.

In 1950, I was graduated from Pratt with honors and entered the field of advertising design. My prewar studies in graphics in Warsaw provided an added dimension in allowing me to achieve a high standard of professionalism. Soon after graduation, I was privileged to work with and befriend one of the giants of American graphic design, the world-renowned Paul Rand, whose work greatly influenced me. Over the years, our warm professional relationship deepened into a close friendship, which we enjoyed as well with his gracious wife, Marion.

I was also reunited with Professor Tadeusz Lipski—who

had moved to New York—who had taught me paper sculpture and three-dimensional design at the Piłsudski School. We collaborated on many creative projects together, and our friendship continued until his death in 1987.

Over the years, I established my own freelance design studio and worked for several leading American and international corporations. In addition, by offering my services as a designer and consultant, I was able to express my gratitude to various philanthropic organizations and institutions that had helped me in the postwar years. Among other rewarding activities, I taught calligraphy and paper sculpture at the School of Visual Arts in New York.

In 1952, I married Helen Rosenberg, who had survived the war in Poland with her parents, Agatha and Józef Rosenberg. They were saved by an elderly couple, noble Christians who risked their own lives by hiding them and shielding them for sixteen months in their little house on the outskirts of their home town Żółkiew, near Lwów. Helen's devotion to her parents made a powerful impression on me.

We were blessed with two children. Diane, a doctor of clinical psychology, is married to Chaim Zlotogorski, a son of survivors of Auschwitz. They have three sons, Yonatan Yosef, David Pesach, and Yehoshua Shlomo. Barry, a biomedical engineer, is married to Yael London. They also have three children, Ruth Esther, Avraham Yosef, and Adi Tova.

What we, the survivors, were forced to see and experience was so evil that I sometimes think we should not be able to live a normal life and enjoy anything any more. On the other hand, we came so close to witnessing the end of the Jewish people that we have the great responsibility to tell the world what happened to us. This is what kept me alive.

I offer a fervent prayer that Shalom, a lasting peace, should prevail, that the words of the prophet Isaiah should become a reality for us survivors of genocide, for the State of Israel, and for all peoples of the world.

Poster by the author commemorating his survival from summary execution in Budzyń, 1943.
Designed at Pratt Institute, New York, 1948

Afterword

    This extraordinary memoir by Morris Wyszogrod is an account of his journey through vastly different worlds. Unlike inanimate objects that are merely in a world, it can be said that human beings have a world, act upon it, build, and change it. Such a world, for example, that of the artist, the engineer, or the mathematician, is embedded in a deeper frame of reference—what philosopher Edmund Husserl called a life-world, the taken-for-granted reality of our daily environment that is reliable for all practical purposes. The world of the concentration camps emerges as a systematic effort to destroy the life-world, the sphere in which the micro-practices that make human existence possible are enacted. Here the very scaffolding of experience itself is dismantled.

    The many worlds of Morris Wyszogrod, a Jewish artist born in Poland, whose experiences in the Warsaw Ghetto and in concentration camps Majdanek (briefly as a transfer point), Budzyń, Płaszów, Zschachwitz (a camp near Dresden), and finally Theresienstadt, confront the reader with a story of events that could not have been imagined had they not in fact actually occurred. With the Nazi invasion of Poland, Morris Wyszogrod was cut off for a long period from the rich heritage of religious learning, political ideals, and cultural activities that constituted the ambiance of Polish Jewry, one that had sustained his personal and artistic development. At the same time, the war also compelled him to sever his ties to Polish art circles that had already absorbed new trends derived from Western European art and had provided a matrix of forms and techniques that could only excite a budding artist.

The present work describes his passage through contrasting spheres of experience. There is first the world of the gifted art student born into a loving and cultivated Warsaw Jewish family with a passion for music. As a young man he is cast into a Polish environment that was hostile at worst, indifferent at best, to his aspirations but still allowed for the development of his talents. He is then thrown into the vastly diminished world of the Warsaw ghetto, a sealed-off enclave of violence, disease, and death that was created in November, 1940. Later still, he is caught up in what has sometimes been called the "concentration camp universe," an all-encompassing environment of death. From the immediate postwar period to the present he has been working as a graphic designer, calligrapher, and paper sculptor, a life that enables him to depict the images of the camps in which he had been imprisoned and from which he felt himself to have been miraculously liberated.

The claim that it is impossible to create art works after Auschwitz has become a critical commonplace. Had not

Theodor Adorno written, "To write poetry after Auschwitz is barbaric"?[1] Two quite different and incompatible grounds are offered for this impossibility. First, it is objected on moral grounds that Holocaust art aestheticizes atrocities converting them into visual or linguistic artifacts that sanitize the horror of the event. The world of the camps is converted into a stage set for fictionalization whether verbal or visual. Behind the impulse to create Holocaust art is the hope that what happened can somehow be controlled by giving it form and shape. Second, it is objected, such art is impossible on grounds having to do with the nature of the Holocaust itself. Language and image must fail because the violence, the brutality, of the camp system and the emotions of the victims cannot be transformed into a structure of symbolic references; the magnitude of the horror of the event precludes such transposition. Theologian and novelist Arthur Cohen referred to the holocaust as the *tremendum:*

> I call the death camps the *tremendum,* for it is the monument of a meaningless inversion of life to an orgiastic celebration of death, to a psychosexual and pathological degeneracy unparalleled and unfathomable to any person bonded to life.[2]

If what happened had no form or shape, Holocaust literary works and visual art works, it could be contended, must fail.

The power of these arguments rests on the notion that the Holocaust is a single event, the obverse of the holy as it were, and cannot be understood because the nihil, the cataclysm, transcends our powers of cognition or description. This perspective must be honored; if we try to envisage the Holocaust as a totality, it defies depiction. Yet, in fact, the world of the death camps was not the result of the interplay of anonymous social, economic, and political forces but the

237

conscious project of a Nazi leadership dedicated to the annihilation of those it had designated as subhuman, a project implemented with the cooperation of ordinary Germans and assisted by others, largely the inhabitants of Nazi-occupied Eastern European countries. Thus the Holocaust can be seen as encompassing myriad day-to-day happenings, each incident of gratuitous Nazi cruelty having a specificity and concreteness that can be conveyed, yet, at the same time, each event telling us something about all the others. Their cumulative weight may be overwhelming yet, as survivors have proclaimed, each episode demands recounting. If the historian were to refrain from constructing a narrative about these events and rendering judgments about their importance, it would be impossible to say "Thus it was."

Memories may be recorded visually and orally on videotape that, unlike the written memoir, carries with it the hesitations and missteps of living speech and captures the affective registers of the survivor as he or she relives the remembered events. The written memoir on the other hand allows for reflection and the correction of first impressions. Neither purports to be a work of art but, to the contrary, each reflects an effort to avoid narrative transformation or embellishment. While the survivor is neither a historian nor a moral philosopher, he or she, like the historian, hopes to offer a chronicle of what happened and, at the same time, like the moral philosopher to arouse ethical reflection about the events depicted. But the visual artist cannot replicate the past in the manner of the camera whose purpose it is to capture the image of an event as seen by the photographer through the camera's viewfinder, an image that can then become material for further historical articulation. For even if the artist means to lay hold of a specific moment, to represent it as a living presence, the art work by its very nature enters into a context of aesthetic

238

interpretation that will determine some of the meanings contemporary and future viewers ascribe to it. In addition, it has been a shibboleth of modern art that good art cannot be didactic, that it cannot subordinate itself to a moral message but must be appreciated for its formal properties. The artist, unlike the philosopher, it has been argued, does not as an artist enter into debates about ethical issues even if he or she may wish to do so in some other capacity. While the assertion that art is neither history nor moral philosophy has been the subject of extended discussion prior to the Holocaust, paradoxes generated by the horror of the Holocaust have raised the stakes inherent in this debate.

As I have noted earlier, the Holocaust survivor has been forced to choose between a silence that would erase the particularity of his or her experience consigning it to oblivion or a speaking out that could never adequately convey the world of death that the individual had survived. The latter alternative, telling it as it was, the promise of verisimilitude, demands that the writer reach down into memory, relive the terror and pain of that world, cross and recross the chasm separating current life from the unthinkable domain of death. What is more, even if the memoirist is not writing fiction, it is still necessary to reach for metaphors, for figures of speech, that will allow the reader as little escape as possible from the reality of the Holocaust and, in so doing, to a certain extent, turn life into literature. When language has force—even when it is as spare and austere as that of Franz Kafka, Samuel Beckett, or Jorge Luis Borges—it aestheticizes the phenomenon it depicts. Who could fail to be moved by the power of the words in Paul Celan's "Death Fugue," a poem that is seen by many commentators as *the* poem of the Holocaust (if this expression were not somehow self-contradictory). Celan writes, "Black milk of daybreak we drink you at night / we

239

drink you at noon in the morning we drink you at sundown /
we drink and we drink you."[3]

The survivor seeks to chronicle experience, to devise a
language of maximum transparency, a language that, like
glass, will enable the viewer to see through it to the events
being recounted rather than to transform experience poet-
ically. How, it may be asked, can this aim be achieved? Can the
memoirist appeal to the once potent symbols of myth and
tradition in order to illuminate the horror of the events
depicted, perhaps even to derive meaning from them? And if
it is not possible to appeal to a reservoir of traditional symbols
to do so, can the survivor find language that will suggest "the
sound and the fury signifying nothing," the nihil, the cataclysm that is the death world of the Holocaust?

This problem of the loss of meaning in the context of
the destruction of European civilization is suggested in
Aharon Appelfeld's novel, *In the Land of the Cattails,* the story
of an ominous journey of a mother and son who, just prior to
the outbreak of World War II, set out from Austria to travel
eastward across what would become the sites of mass murder,
death camps, and killing fields. Appelfeld exposes the illusion that culture can constrain brutality. In one memorable
scene that takes place in a railway car, the novel depicts a
conversation in the presence of the novel's hero between a
woman and an unknown gentleman of aristocratic appearance. The woman sighs nostalgically:

> "If I had studied painting I wouldn't be living here. I would be
> living in Rome."
> "Why Rome?" The tall man expressed his surprise in a re-
> strained voice.
> "There all of mankind's treasures are laid up, freedom,
> beauty, everything that is lacking here."[4]

240

She expresses the ineluctable yearning for what she believes renders life meaningful, yet earlier in the narrative when the same woman expressed the optimistic view that all would be well in the end, the strange man punctured her illusion. "Where will that wellness come from?" he asks. When she suggested, "from within," her answer could be seen as making no sense in the context of a world on the verge of collapse.[5]

If the power of myth and tradition has been eroded as a resource for articulating meaning and value, is it possible, one might ask, for a survivor to find in his or her métier or profession symbols to help convey the sense of what happened, a language whose metaphors can be deployed to depict the holocaustal universe? In his various reflections on the Holocaust, Primo Levi, a chemist before, during, and after the war, appeals to the figures of speech used in his profession and to those of its prescientific predecessor, medieval alchemy whose aim was to transform base metal into gold. It can be argued that Levi uses the allusion to alchemy to suggest a reversal of the process, the transformation from a world of ordinary existence to that of the Holocaust.[6]

Yet metaphors derived from the familiar world of everyday experience pull the reader back into a certain normalcy. What is more, because his scientific training saved Primo Levi's life in that his skills were deemed useful by the Nazis, a reader of his various memoirs might be led to believe, misleadingly, that even there, in the camps, there was an enclave of sanity. The relation of Morris Wyszogrod's art to the Holocaust may lead the reader to confront a somewhat similar dilemma to that suggested by Levi's story because, like Levi, Wyszogrod's work emanates from several entirely different situations, the first, work produced in response to the orders of the Nazi guards and camp officials and the second, work created in the pre and postwar periods.

If the literary and artistic resources I have mentioned have serious limitations, are we not compelled to ask whether all attempts to convey the full horror of what happened by visual and narrative means are bound to fail? To concede this point would be to surrender the recounting of events to the unscrupulous creators of lies, who either deny the Holocaust outright or intentionally distort its character. Instead, the language of Holocaust narrative must be seen as saying more than it says, as being doubly coded—that is, as conveying two messages: for each and every description that suggests a remnant of ordinary life, there is always another meaning that accompanies it, death, nothingness, annihilation. Thus, the camp system could always rebound and punish with immense ferocity the same act that it had rewarded. If one were a chemist, an artist, or an engineer, and at the same time an inmate, a nonperson, then one must be punished for daring to exhibit the skills of professions that were seen by the Nazi camp personnel to belong to the masters. Similarly camp language conveys not only the standard meanings of terms but also their opposites. The word *food* in everyday existence means nourishment and perhaps the conviviality of a shared meal, but in the concentration camp, where death is pandemic, an opposite meaning, decay and death, attaches itself like a ghost to the ordinary one. Camp food, even if nauseating and insubstantial, is still sustenance but, alongside this meaning, there lurks the threat of death by starvation through the withdrawal of even this basic nourishment.

For the visual artist who attempts to illustrate the Nazi regime of terror, images can capture the sadism and brutality that governed Nazi practices from the creation of Jewish ghettos, to the conditions governing the deportation of vast numbers of persons, to life in the camps themselves. But visual art cannot unaided provide a context for these images.

What is more, the fact that art is displayed through a style may, contrary to the artist's intention, determine the character of the images it exhibits and, by calling attention to itself, lessen the moral horror it hopes to communicate. Consider the case of some gifted painters and graphic artists who were somehow able to obtain art supplies and to continue working in the Terezin ghetto prior to the deportations of the ghetto's inhabitants. Images of ghetto life created by Bedrich Fritta (Fritz Taussig), Otto Ungar, Felix Bloch, and Leo Haas[7] were hidden by the artists and subsequently recovered after the war by those who survived. But despite the efforts of these talented artists to convey what they saw, their works cannot help displaying a largely modernist aesthetic in that modernism was the artistic idiom in which they were schooled.

The viewer thus is led to see these works in terms of a system of references to other works, for example, the Paris street scenes of Maurice Utrillo, the peasants of Pierre Bonnard, or the anguished faces of Edvard Munch, so that the despair specific to life in the ghetto is, to an extent, mitigated. A case in point is the remarkable depiction of a café in Terezin by the gifted artist Leo Haas, which could easily be misinterpreted as simply a scene of modernist angst. Therefore art, like the Holocaust memoir, must be understood as having a double signification. On the one hand the art work may be viewed as a formal articulation of visual values but, on the other, it requires an accompanying narrative to establish its context. The artist or the custodian of Holocaust artifacts who wishes images to convey not only an event but the circumstances from which it emerged, may be compelled to abandon the modernist aesthetic which demands that we see only pure form in order to coerce the image into speech. Morris Wyszogrod's images of gratuitous brutality as they are reproduced in the present memoir are not only stark images of cruelty but are embedded in a narrative that contextualizes the visual material and intensifies its moral force.

Much has been written about post-Holocaust art and architecture dedicated to the memory of the victims by those of succeeding generations who were not themselves part of the event. What could and could not be said or shown aroused heated controversy. The disputes surrounding the site, architecture, and content of the Holocaust Museum in Washington, D.C., and of the Jewish Memorial Museum designed by Daniel Liebeskind for a site in Berlin have been widely publicized and I shall not enter into details of these polemics here. Yet it is difficult to contest the overwhelming emotional impact of such works as the memorial sculpture at Majdanek, one of the camps in which Morris Wyszogrod had been briefly interned. The sculpture erected in 1976 by Wiktor Tolkin and Janusz Dembek exhibits hollows and curves somewhat reminiscent of the works of Henry Moore. But its effect results not so much from the formal relation of its parts as from the fact that the crematoria, guard towers, and a mausoleum covering the ashes of the dead are visible through an aperture at the base of the sculpture.[8] Similarly, the chalk-white, prone figures of George Segal's monumental Holocaust memorial sculpture in the San Francisco Legion of Honor Museum derives its emotional impact in no small measure from the narrative context supplied by the exhibit itself and from the fact that the death imagery of the Holocaust, however inadequate to the event itself, has become a part of the historical background against which we live.

But the dilemmas presented by Morris Wyszogrod's work are different from those posed by post-Holocaust memorial art because, as I noted earlier, he was not separated from his métier in the camps. When officials of the work brigades and later of the concentration camps learned of his talents, he was immediately recruited to create portraits of the wives and sweethearts of the guards and other personnel, to decorate the rooms of the children of Nazi families, and to devise pornographic settings for the sexual activities of the guards. Yet the talent that saved his life also placed him in constant danger, for unlike the science of chemistry, Primo Levi's field of expertise, the work of the artist may be dangerously ambiguous and can be interpreted as constituting a threat to those in charge. What is more, he was able to observe the intimate lives of camp personnel at close range and in a manner usually denied to most inmates. In sum, the relation of Morris Wyszogrod's art to the Holocaust is complicated by the fact that he not only illustrated events in the camps as he remembered them after the war but that, as an inmate perceived by the Nazis as "subhuman," he became artist on call, as it were, in the camps where he was held, creating works for his SS masters under the threat of death. Known as "Kunst-mahler" to the SS, his works were in steady demand.

Some might argue that graphics produced under these conditions to meet arbitrary specifications cannot be called art. Yet, it could also be asked, does art not operate under imperatives that mandate excellence and can such excellence not be construed as a way to surmount the brutality of the world in which the artist was forced to move? If the answer is negative, then value is denied to such works, yet if it is positive, one is subject to an even more significant danger. For were these works to be recovered and artistic merit ascribed to them, the fact that interesting art could have emerged from the camps might be viewed as somehow justifying a diminished sense of outrage at the conditions under which they were created. Thus the reader of this memoir is challenged at every turn by the most difficult questions concerning the relation of art to ethics and the place of art in human existence.

Morris Wyszogrod's works reproduced here, postwar sketches of events that occurred in the camps (some of which are copies of drawings from the immediate postwar period), forces the reader to ponder these questions. Once a context is established by the written text, the sketches avoid the ambiguity that attaches to a visual work that is unaccompanied by narrative; at the same time the narrative context opens up the images so that they become a moral commentary upon the events they depict. Thus there is a tension in the Holocaust artwork between aesthetic and ethical considerations, a tension that is, indeed must be, subordinated to the moral power of the narrative, as the horrors revealed in this account make us see.

I have refrained from discussing the specific happenings described in this memoir. That can and must only be told by Morris Wyszogrod in his own distinctive way. His depiction of the world of the camps, it must be confessed, has a special hold on my imagination not only because I know the author and his family and count them as close friends but also because the coincidence of names (Wyschogrod is my name through marriage) creates a strange existential bond. In pondering this coincidence, I am reminded of the tale told about Gautama the Buddha who, upon emerging from the sheltered environment of his father's palace, sees for the first time, an old man, a diseased man, and finally a corpse. When confronted by the world's ills, old age, disease, and death from which he heretofore had been elaborately shielded, the young prince expresses with precision my own altered sense of things after reading and reflecting upon this memoir when he asks in despair, "Could this too happen to me?"

Edith Wyschogrod
Rice University

NOTES

1. Theodor W. Adorno, *Prisms*, trans. Samuel and Shierry Weber (Cambridge: MIT Press, 1986), p. 34.

2. Arthur A. Cohen, *The Tremendum: A Theological Interpretation of the Holocaust* (New York: Crossroads, 1981), p. 19.

3. Paul Celan, *Poems of Paul Celan*, trans. Michael Hamburger (New York: Persea Books, 1988), p. 61.

4. Aharon Appelfeld, *To the Land of the Cattails*, trans. Jeffrey M. Green, (New York: Weidenfeld and Nicolson, 1986), p. 145.

5. Ibid., p. 143.

6. See Primo Levi, *Survival in Auschwitz*, trans. Stuart Woolf, (New York: Collier Books, 1973) and *The Monkey's Wrench*, trans. William Weaver (New York: Summit Books, 1986).

7. Lawrence Langer, *Art from the Ashes*, ed. (New York: Oxford University Press, 1995). See pp. 670–75 for reproductions of their works.

8. Photographs of the Majdanek monument together with an explanatory text, both by James E. Young, can be found in his *Writing and Rewriting the Holocaust: Narratives and the Consequences of Interpretation* (Bloomington: Indiana University Press, 1988), p. 153.

Index of Names

N.B.: References to photographs and illustrations are in italics.

A
Aaron Krelman School 17
Ackerman, Jacob 17
Alexandra (Soviet nurse) 212
Alfred (cook, Okęcie) 51, 52
Aliberti (doctor) 197
American Jewish Joint Distribution
  Committee (JDC) 66, 223, 224,
  225, 226
Anatol 200
Arbus, Isak 145, 151
Auschwitz 181, 185, 223
Axmann, Adolf 157, 163, 164, 170

B
Baron, Naphtali 18
Bauchwitz, Rudi 163, 164, *165*
Ber 27
Beregszasz, Hungary 185

Berlin 172, 224
Bieda brothers 67
Bielany (*Centralny Instytut
  Wychowania Fizycznego*) 34, 36
Bielenki (doctor) 110
Bitter 158, 159, *160–161,* 162,
Bizewski (*Zugwachman*) 125
Blaifeder, Esther (cousin) 229
Blaifeder, Faige (aunt) 228, 229
Blaifeder, Martin (cousin) 229
Blaifeder, Mendel. *See* Blajfeder,
  Mendel (uncle)
Blaifeder, Morris (cousin) 229
Blajfeder, Bela (aunt) 25, 84, 106,
  110
Blajfeder, Boruch (uncle) 8, 15,
  91, 101, 150
Blajfeder, Chana (cousin, Yankel's
  daughter) 100

Blajfeder, Chana (cousin, Boruch's daughter) 101
Blajfeder, Chana Riva (grandfather's second wife) 4
Blajfeder, David (cousin) 8, 31, 101
Blajfeder, Doba (mother) 3, *6*
Blajfeder, Esther Gincel (maternal grandmother) 3, 4
Blajfeder, Eva (aunt) 101
Blajfeder, Frimet (aunt) 100
Blajfeder, Hershel (uncle) 8, 100
Blajfeder, Isser (uncle) 101, 102
Blajfeder, Itzchak (uncle) 18, 28, 31
Blajfeder, Justina (aunt) 101
Blajfeder, Malka (aunt) 31
Blajfeder, Mendel (uncle) 4, 15, 16, 86, 223, 228, 229
Blajfeder, Miriam (aunt) 100
Blajfeder, Moshe (cousin) 8, 31, 100, 105
Blajfeder, Moshe Halevi ben Yekutiel (maternal grandfather) 3
Blajfeder, Pesa Drajer (aunt) 10, 27, 29, 84, 86, 105
Blajfeder, Velvel (uncle) 52, 53, 100
Blajfeder, Yankel (uncle) 100
"Borscht," *see also Malpe* 129, *130*, 215
Boudreau, James C. 230
Brandt (*Obersturmfuehrer*) 117, 118, 121
Braun, Gabriel 2
Brown (musician) 218
Buchenholz, Kurt 198, 200, 214
Buchenholz, Pauline 214
Budzyń 84, 124, 126, 128, 131, 133, *134*, 136, *140*, 143, 145, 146, 150, 153, *160–161*, 162, 163, *165*, 170, 179, 208, 215
Bug River 30
Bulkowstein, Sasha 139

Buseck, Freiherr von 43, 44, 80
Bykowski, Bronisław 19, 20, 119

C
Callaghan, Irene Murray 230
Cetnarowski, Antoni 21
Chajkin (male nurse) 145
Chilewicz 188
Cliff 200
Cohen, Moshe 139
Concentration Camps (map) *114*
Cracow 187, 191
Cylich, Ruth 223
Cylich, Samuel 223, 224
Czapnik, Noah 75, 76

D
Dąbrowski, Stanisław 20, 21, 33, 39, 41
Debernitz 37, 38
Der Geyler Mordche 147, 213
Der Geyler Paltn 13
Dorfsman, Yitzhak 155, 189
Dos hentl 103
Drajer, Avraham Mendel 27, 29, 72, 84, 105, 124
Drajer, Leib 124, 125, 214
Drajer, Pesa. *See* Blajfeder, Pesa
Drajer, Moshe 27, 105
Dresden 26, 195, 197, 199, 201, 203, 206
Dzielna Street 4, 116, 219

E
Edelsbourgh, Henry 223
Eisenberg, Aaron 42, 48, 49, 50, 51, 52, 55, 79, 87
Elektoralna Street 78
Eljowicz, Jacob 152, 178, 215
Engelman, Bolesław 19
Erich (BV) 193

F
Falk, S. 144
Feinberg (doctor) 223

Feix, Reinhold 128, 129, *130*, 131, 133, *134*, 137, 141, 142, 145, 151, 157, 158, 159, 163, 167, 169, 170, 174, 215
Ferdinand (prisoner, Zschachwitz) 200
Fischer (*Obergefreiter*) 90, 91
Fischer, Karl 56
Fischer, Otto 46
Flamm, Golde 103
Flamm, Josef Dov 18, 103, 119, 152, 204
Flasterstein, Yankel 69, 124
Flato, Stanley 139, *140*, 141
Flossenbürg, Bavaria 195
Foerster (doctor) 145, 151
Fritz (BV, Zschachwitz) 200, 207

G
Gęsia Street 8, 88, 109, 125, 221
Gershberg 223
Gingold, David 89, 106, 107, 108
Gincel, Esther 3
Glatstein, Hanoch 112, 113, 120
Glatstein, Mordechai 112, 113, 120, 122
Glatstein (horse-cart driver) 146
Goldman, Adam 120
Goldman, Peretz 120
Goeth, Amon 188
Graf family 218
Gram, Yehuda 146, 147, 185, 192
Grochowski, Jerzy 206
Grosman family 189
Gross (doctor) 192
Gross-Rosen 181
Gruszka brothers 51
Grynberg, David 120, 144, 208
Grzybowska Street 41
Gutmacher 83

H
Handtke 131
Hannelore 166
Heinkel Werke 136, 149, 183, 184

Hentze 172
Hochrad, Szyja 151, 181
Hoycher Moyshe 25
Hrubieszów, Poland 181
Hujowa Góra 189

I
Ishchenko, Fiodor Pavlovich 223, 224
Ivan (BV) 190, 191
Iven (*Stabsfeldwebel*) 80, 81, 109, 110, 111, 113

J
Jabotinsky, Zev 16
Jaeger, Karl 150, 153, 172
Jarniewski, Samuel 149, 152
Jarząb, Jan 21
JDC. *See* American Jewish Joint Distribution Committee
Judenrat 32, 33, 41, 42, 53, 66, 68, 79, 117

K
Kamiński, Kazimierz 219
Katz 90
Kava, Pesach 167
Kershaw, David 230
Kershaw, Eva 204, 205, 230
Kershaw, Murray 230
Kessel, Moshe 123
Kielce 225
Kirszencweig 27
Klauss (*Unterscharfuehrer*) 155
Konwiktorska Street 222
Kornblum, Itzchak 19, 22
Koussevitsky, Sergei 12
Kozłowski 104
Kraśnik 143, 167, 178, 189
Krebs 198
Kutno, Pomerania 42

L
Lachman, Mayer 120, 133, 181

Lasko 223
Lawrusiewicz 14
Leipold (*Untersturmfuehrer*) 174, 175, 177, 178, 179, 182
Leipzig 77
Leitmeritz, Sudetenland 206, 207, 208, 209, 215
Leszno Street 82, 87, 89
Lewinson (violinist) 82
Lewitan (musician) 10, 12
Lewitan (Warsaw lawyer) 172
Licht 103, 104, 107, 108, 109, 115, 123
Lichtenstein (Warsaw Jew) 202
Lindeke, Hermann 77, 78, 79
Lipski, Tadeusz 20, 230
Łódź 66, 115, 148, 216, 217
Lubicz 18
Lublin, 89, 124, 170, 172, 177, 226
Lustman 13
Lwów 182

M
Majdanek 124, 126, 170
Malpe (Ape), *see also* "Borscht" 129, *130*, 215
Mandel, Josef 198, 205
Mandelbaum, Izak 12, 13, 16
Mandeltort, Mark 51, 111
Marks (*Feldwebel*) 115, 117
Marshal Józef Piłsudski School of Graphics 19, 20, 22, 24, 33, 106, 222, 231
Marx (*Feldwebel*) 196, 197
Maus (*Obergefreiter*) 76, 80
Meissner, Arthur 202
Meyer *Kocioł* 146
Miag Werke 195, *202*
Michaiło (Ukrainian guard) 173
Miła Street 106, 110
Mława 55
Mohr 170, 171
Mosbach, Erich 145, 159, 179, 182
Mossakowski, Eugeniusz 13

N
Nalewki Street 14
Niska Street 106, 107, 108
Nissenbaum 150
Nowolipie Street 100, 101, 102, 116
Nowolipki Street 18, 84, 116

O
Okęcie 42, 87, 100, 107, 108, 115, 123, 144, 208, 215
Okopowa Street 108
Oranienburg 181
Orlik (doctor) 206, 207
ORT (Organization for Rehabilitation through Training) 8
Otto (Ukrainian platoon leader) 137, 159

P
Paul (prisoner, Zschachwitz) 200
Paris 61, 62, 226
Pawia Street 4, 14, 41, 52, 117, 220, *221*
Pawiak prison 4, 5, 219
Penciak, Bolesław 21, 41, 222
Płaszów 187, 188, 191, 195
Polakov (Ukrainian guard) 158, 159
Pommerenke, Willi 43, 44, 45, 47, 48, 50, 51, 59, 75, 77, 79, 80, 96, 98
Poniatowa 124, 170
Popov (Ukrainian guard) 159
Posner (rabbi) 144
Praga 220, 222, 224
Prague 207, 213
Pratt Institute 227, 230
Próchniak 79, 104, 112, 113
Przejazd Street 59
Pupko, S. 84, 128

R
Radom 118, 121, 181
Rand, Marion 230

Rand, Paul 230
Rigman, Moshe. See *der Geyler Paltn* 13
Rinde, Chiel 117, 118, 120
Ringelblum, Emmanuel 18
Rose family 78, 79
Rosenberg, Agatha 231
Rosenberg, Helen 231
Rosenberg, Józef 231
Rosenstrauch, Zosia 37
Rosenthal, David 144
Rosner brothers 188
Rostock, Germany 152
Rozen 38
Rubin, Izak 24, 60, 72, 86, 170
Ruzicka, Thomas 230

S
Sagh, Alexander (Sandor) 185, 195, 196, 197, 198, 204, 205
Sagh, Eva. *See* Kershaw, Eva
Sagh, Simon 185, 195, 196, 197, 198, 199, 204, 205, 206, 207, 215, 230
Saint Augustine Church 4, 5, 27, 116, 219
Salt mines. *See* Wieliczka
Sasse (*Unteroffizier*) 48
Scherschneider, Bernard 61, 227
Scherschneider, Lillian 226, 227
School of Visual Arts 231
Schragner (*SS Unterscharfuehrer*) 154, 155, 170, 179, 180, 184, 185
Schultze (Lieutenant) 103, 104, 107, 109, 110
Shura. *See* Alexandra
Simcha ("the mobile cafeteria") 13
Smocza Street 116, 219, 220, 221
Sommer (barber) 182
Sołtan, Aleksander 21
Spier, Jo 210
Stepan (naval officer) 152, 172
Stockhammer (rabbi) 144

Stockman, Noah 127, 149, 163, 166, 167, 169
Stromberg (clarinetist) 82
Stettin 226
Stolinski 55, 56
Świątkowski, Antoni Andrzej 75
Świętojerska Street 100, 105
Świętosławski, Henryk 42
Szeroka Street 220, 222
Szersznajder, Berele. *See* Scherschneider, Bernard
Szerman family 12, 62
   Aaron 12
   Sholem 12
   Tsalke 12
Sznaj, Chaim 216, 217
Sztajnkalk, Zygmunt 84
Sztyleryt, Berl 42
Szulc, Roman 12
Szumański (professor) 218
Szyfryn, Zofia 71, 83, 84

T
Targowa Street 222
Tauscher (SS *Untersturmfuehrer*) 170, 171, 173, 175, 199, 206
Theresienstadt 209, 210, 213, 214, 216
Topas, Jurek (George) 107, 108, 109, 120
Trawniki 124, 170
Treblinka 76, 89, 101, 106
Trout, Jonathan 230
Tscherny, George 230
Tychowski, Wiktor 14, 58
Tylbor, Henry 144
Tylbor, Rubin 144

U
Umschlagplatz 89, 90, 91, 108, 115, 116, 117, *118*
Uprising, Polish (August 1944) 27, 206
Uprising, Warsaw ghetto
   January 1943 106

Uprising, Warsaw ghetto
(*continued*)
April 1943 110, 125
Urias, Edmundo Rodolfo 230

V
Vetter (*Unterscharfuehrer*) 157, 164, 167, 170
Vickum 46
Vistula River 8, 221

W
Wajnberg 27, 89, 90
Wallant, Edward 230
Warsaw Ghetto (map) *64*
Warszawski, Amram 19, 37
Warszawski, Yakir 19
Wieliczka 182, 184
Wierchowska, Zofia 13, 58, 85
Wierzbowski 222
Wischogrod, Moses 46
Wołynska Street 61, 102
Wyshogrod, Adi Tova (grand-daughter) 231
Wyshogrod, Avraham Yosef (grandson) 231
Wyshogrod, Barry (son) 231
Wyshogrod, Ruth Esther (grand-daughter) 231
Wyshogrod, Yael London (daughter-in-law) 231
Wyszegrod, Abraham Joseph (cousin) 226
Wyszegrod, Basia (aunt) 2
Wyszegrod, Hirsh Baer (uncle) 2, 226
Wyszegrod, Josef (uncle) 2, 8
Wyszegrod, Mordechai Leib (cousin) 8, 15, 86
Wyszogrod, Chaim Boruch (father) 1, *6*, 124, 227
Wyszogrod, Esther Raizl (sister) 4, *6*, 10, 84, 214

Wyszogród, Mieczysław (Polish ver-sion of author's name) 216
Wyszogrod, Mordechai (grand-father) 1
Wyszogrod, Moshe Mordechai (Hebrew version of author's name) 223
Wyszogród, Mojzesz (Polish ver-sion of author's name) 220
Wyszogrod, Pesach (brother) 4, *6*, 10, *11*, 42, 62, 70, 82, 84, 85, 91, 100, 101, 102, 103, 104, 105, 106, 109, 110, 111, 119, 125, 214
Wyszogrod, Shlomo Yitzhak (brother) 4, *6*, 10, *11*, 81, 84, 86, 214

Y
Yesayef (doctor) 212, 214
Yossl (musician) 219

Z
Zając 83, 84
Zaleski 72, 73, 74, 225, 226
Zamenhofa Street 106, 108
Zdzisno, Lithuania 146
Żelazna Street 116
Ziemba (rabbi) 144
Złoto, Naftali 74, 75, 85, 113, 118
Zlotogorski, Chaim (son-in-law) 231
Zlotogorski, David Pesach (grand-son) 231
Zlotogorski, Diane Wyshogrod (daughter) 231
Zlotogorski, Yehoshua Shlomo (grandson) 231
Zlotogorski, Yonatan Yosef (grand-son) 231
Żółkiew 231
Zschachwitz, Germany 195, 197, 200, 207